Tricky Latin

Puzzles

Julian Morgan

DEDICATION

For Christine and Ines
(alpha and omega)

ACKNOWLEDGEMENTS

My special thanks go to Irini Sevastaki,
who helped in checking the manuscript of this book.

CONTENTS

Introduction   Page 1

Puzzles   Page 2

Solutions   Page 74

Also Available   Page 84

About the Author   Page 90

Introduction

The study of Latin is a bit of a puzzle in itself, or rather, a whole long set of them extending towards infinity. It is a highly rewarding and enjoyable process but also challenging, so this is where brainteasers and mind games can help in lightening things up: my first attempt to distribute a set of these came with my book **Easy Latin Puzzles**, which I based on a set of simple word lists and a very limited number of grammatical inflexions. The collection has proved popular and I have been glad to hear that people are enjoying it, as I hope they will continue to do in the future. A recent revision has brought many improvements and seen it expanded to include ten new puzzles.

Tricky Latin Puzzles was first compiled in 2016 in an attempt to raise the bar and now in this latest edition I have made general improvements throughout and have added 15 new puzzles at the back of the collection. The challenge here for the puzzler will be to work some magic using an extended base of vocabulary and word endings. **Tricky Latin Puzzles** is exactly what it says on the cover, I hope, and if you don't find this book at least a little bit difficult, I shall have failed in my task. The book is suitable for those who have studied the language for at least two or three years.

Please note that a recent addition to my range of classical puzzle books is the all-Latin **Quare id faciam**, in which the keen student of the language may be delighted to find *absolutely no English at all!* You can read about this on our website, www.j-progs.com.

Good luck with the puzzles and please email me if you see ways by which I can improve this book or if you have have ideas about other new projects.

julian@j-progs.com

1   Latin to English crossword

The clues are in Latin but your answers should be in English.

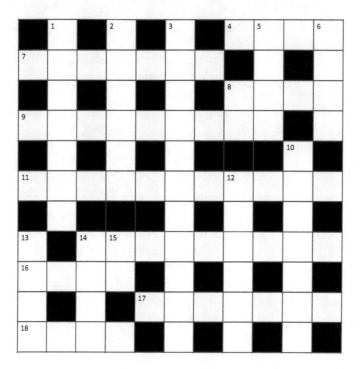

Across

4. Quoque (4)
7. Sum paratus (2,5)
8. Facite (4)
9. Amovimus (2,7)
11. Sis (3,6,2)
14. Perturbans (9)
16. Quam (4)
17. Coniunctione (2,5)
18. Convenire (4)

Down

1. Princeps (7)
2. Exit (6)
3. Audeo laedere (1,4,6)
5. Duc (4)
6. Apertum (4)
8. Nos sine te (2)
10. Relinquere (7)
12. Perdens (6)
13. Stirps (4)
14. Venit (4)
15. In (2)

2　English to Latin crossword

The clues are in English but your answers should be in Latin.

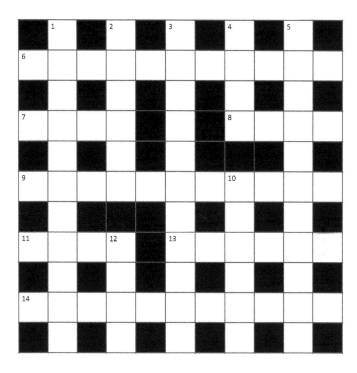

Across

6. They rose (11)
7. You approach (4)
8. Dice (4)
9. Of health (11)
11. Terrible woman (4)
13. I bear witness (6)
14. Of the horrific event (11)

Down

1. Forty (11)
2. A sad thing (6)
3. On purpose (2,9)
4. Weapons (4)
5. In the middle once (2,5,4)
10. He stands in (6)
12. Love (4)

3   Latin to Latin crossword

The clues are in Latin and your answers should also be in Latin.

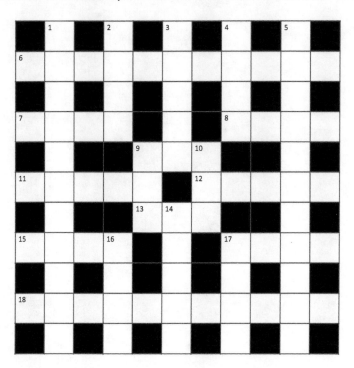

Across

6. Repellere (11)
7. Verres (4)
8. Unus est, plures … (4)
9. Fias (3)
11. Poscit (5)
12. Quae nimium vini bibit? (5)
13. Summa in urbe (3)
15. Quomodo bonum faciatur (4)
17. Non aperte (4)
18. Quod iam erit (4,7)

Down

1. Filius Achillis (11)
2. Donavi (4)
3. Negavi (5)
4. Litora (4)
5. Imperium Augustorum (11)
9. Noli sedere (3)
10. Intra quinque et septem (3)
14. Non frequens (5)
16. Vide (4)
17. Unum crurum (4)

4   Famous Romans: Aeneas

See if you can complete the grid below and by so doing, find out the expression which goes down the middle of the grid.

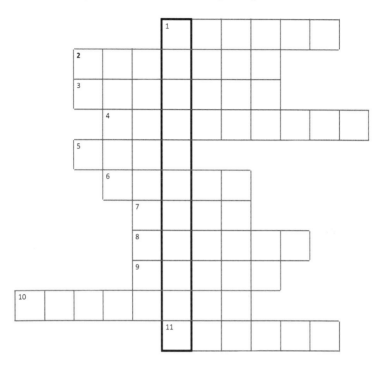

1.   He appeared in a dream instructing Aeneas to leave Troy (6)
2.   The daughter of Latinus, who became Aeneas' wife (7)
3.   A priest of Neptune whose boys were squished by snakes (7)
4.   A helmsman who fell off his helm (9)
5.   Dido's sister (4)
6.   A special lady from Cumae (5)
7.   AKA by Jupiter (4)
8.   She was Aeneas' first wife (6)
9.   Aeneas' mother (5)
10.   Aeneas' father (8)
11.   King of the Rutuli (6)

The expression is: ....

5   Latin phrases wordsearch

The Latin words and phrases from the list below are often used unchanged in various modern languages. They have all been hidden in the grid and your job is to find them. Words may go across, backwards, up, down or diagonally.

I	S	T	E	R	O	B	I	M	N	I	O
I	T	H	D	T	R	A	N	I	U	N	T
D	A	D	H	O	C	R	P	I	U	V	C
N	T	E	P	A	X	E	E	S	T	I	A
A	U	N	E	D	S	T	R	L	L	N	F
R	S	O	R	E	I	E	P	L	I	O	E
E	Q	N	A	F	V	C	E	N	N	V	D
P	U	A	N	A	A	T	T	O	T	E	E
O	O	U	N	C	A	E	U	L	E	R	I
S	I	Q	U	I	R	I	U	I	R	I	N
U	N	E	M	A	A	N	M	T	I	T	D
D	T	N	L	A	R	E	S	I	M	A	E
O	E	I	T	E	R	M	I	N	U	S	A
M	A	S	A	D	N	A	U	S	E	A	M

AD HOC	INTER ALIA	PER ANNUM
AD NAUSEAM	INTERIM	RARA AVIS
DE FACTO	ET CETERA	SINE QUA NON
IN PERPETUUM	MODUS OPERANDI	STATUS QUO
IN VINO VERITAS	PAX	TERMINUS

6   Sudoku

You know how Sudoku works. All you have to do is to place numbers one to nine in each vertical and horizontal line and then make sure that each number appears once in each of the nine 3x3 squares. The difference here is that this is Roman Sudoku!

You use the numbers as below:

1	2	3	4	5	6	7	8	9
I	II	III	IV	V	VI	VII	VIII	IX

III		VII		VI	VIII	IV		I
	VI					II		
				IX	IV			
V				VII			II	IX
VII			VI		II			III
	III			IV				V
			IX	II				
	VII					I	V	
VIII		II	V	I		IX		VII

7   With love, the end

Try to fit all the Latin words into the grid below. Two of them have been done for you, to get you started.

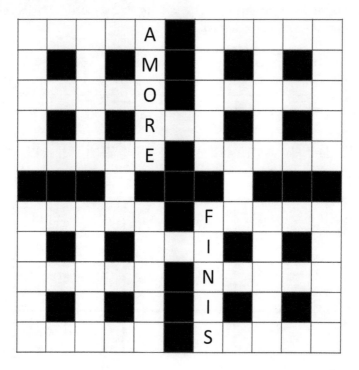

Three letters	Five letters		
MEI	AMARE	GENUS	PECUS
REM	~~AMORE~~	IUSSI	RAMIS
RES	CAPRA	LAPIS	SAEVA
UTI	CESSI	LARGA	SCUTA
	CURAT	NARRO	SISTE
	FINES	NOCTE	STARE
	~~FINIS~~	NOCTU	SUMMA
	GALEA	PALMA	TRAXI

8   Celebration time

Put your answers to the clues in the table below. Some boxes are numbered and where you see these numbers appear elsewhere on this page, they always represent the same letters. Your final job is to reveal a relevant quotation in the table at the bottom.

1	14	12	**2**	17		7	**3**	10		6	11
4	13	10	4	1	11	**5**	10	15		12	8
6	6	17	**7**	2	6	3	2	**8**	17	6	13
9	1	16		6	13	**10**	9	14	1	4	11
11	11	9	2	**12**	5	17	5	2	**13**	11	3	10
14	1	4	6	10	6	13	**15**	11	3	4	10	11
16	2	10	1	4	11	**17**	1	4	10	6
18	13	8	11	2	13	**19**	4	10	12	1	13
20	4	11	**21**	12	11	2	13	**22**	2	3	11
23	7	16	13	4	7	**24**	11	6	6	1	6

1.   Dinner (4)
2.   Wine (5)
3.   Cups (6)
4.   Conquered (Fem.) (8)
5.   To be beaten (Fem.) (8)
6.   I drain (6)
7.   Hurray (4)
8.   Shore (5)
9.   Antony (8)
10.   Victory (8)
11.   Hail (3)
12.   Drink! (Sing.) (4)

13.   Egypt (8)
14.   Victorious procession (9)
15.   Augustus' general (7)
16   Egyptian queen (9)
17.   Of shameful men (7)
18.   Companions (7)
19.   Snakes (9)
20.   Weapons (4)
21.   Ships (5)
22.   Queen (6)
23.   Monster (8)
24.   Emperor (8)

12	6	12	14		2	13	1		5	17	5	2	12	8	6	7

9   Latin to English crossword

The clues are in Latin but your answers should be in English.

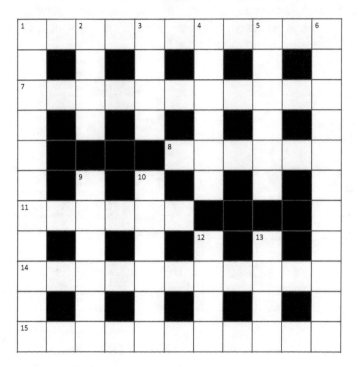

Across

1. Consumpsisse (2,4,5)
7. Intrat sepulcrum (6,1,4)
8. Populus (6)
11. Inspicere (4,2)
14. Heros quidam nonnullis (1,4,2,4)
15. Nihil boni (7,4)

Down

1. Explicant (4,7)
2. Odisse (4)
3. Valde (4)
4. Eradit (6)
5. Copiae (6)
6. Nobilis amicus (5,6)
9. Verberavit (2,4)
10. Tibur (6)
12. Non breve (4)
13. Ire (2,2)

10   English to Latin crossword

The clues are in English but your answers should be in Latin.

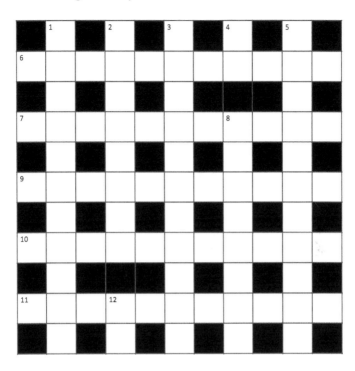

Across

6. On their heads (2,9)
7. Nice favour (5,6)
9. Of a fighter in the arena (11)
10. You did false things (6,5)
11. Claudius' son (11)

Down

1. To understand (11)
2. A clever man (8)
3. A worthy language (6,5)
4. To her (2)
5. His own dagger (5,6)
8. You (Pl.) worship (8)
12. You (Sing.) (2)

11   Latin to Latin crossword

The clues are in Latin and your answers should also be in Latin.

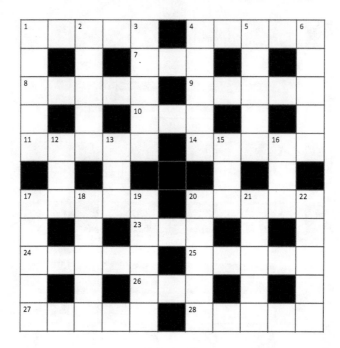

Across

1. Propheta (5)
4. Limitem facio (5)
7. Quodam (3)
8. Non angustum (5)
9. Locus arborum (5)
10. Quod solet (3)
11. Prohibeo (5)
14. Quae omnia cupit (5)
17. Ubi sol non lucet (5)
20. Casae (5)
23. Luce (3)
24. Non aridus (5)
25. Bellum facit? (5)
26. Cedere (3)
27. Rogent (5)
28. Cachinnationem (5)

Down

1. Cupias (5)
2. Omnibus (5)
3. Apice (5)
4. Canalis (5)
5. Non una (5)
6. Obscura (5)
12. Nunc (3)
13. Tribus occasionibus (3)
15. Eheu (3)
16. Contendi (3)
17. Cano quasi lupus (5)
18. Non longum (5)
19. Ne absit (5)
20. Infirmus (5)
21. Terribilis (5)
22. Locatum (5)

12   Crazy, you must know

*The object of the puzzle is to find out which letter of the alphabet is represented by each of the 17 numbers used. You are given two words to start you off, so you can begin by entering any letters from these wherever they appear in the grid. Each word you make should be in good Latin. As you decode each letter, write it in the **Letters deciphered** table and cross it off in the **Letters used** table.*

Letters deciphered

1	2	3	4	5	6	7	8	9	10	11	12	13	14	15	16	17
A	M	E	N	S	C	I	T									

Letters used

13

13   Famous Romans: Cicero

See if you can complete the grid below and by so doing, find out the expression which goes down the middle of the grid.

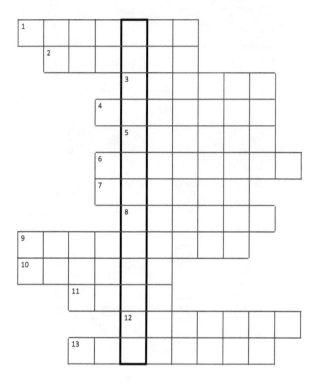

1.   Town where Cicero was born (7)
2.   Caesar's man, Cicero's enemy and Cleopatra's lover (6)
3.   The corrupt governor of a province, prosecuted by Cicero (6)
4.   Cicero's second name (7)
5.   The province referred to in 3. (6)
6.   The original meaning of the name Cicero (8)
7.   The highest rank of state which Cicero reached in 63 BC (6)
8.   Cicero's first name (6)
9.   The social stability which Cicero sought .... ordinum (9)
10.   The "great" triumvir who sometimes lent support to Cicero (6)
11.   Cicero's secretary who invented shorthand (4)
12.   Cicero's best friend and recipient of many of his letters (7)
13.   Chief conspirator who became Cicero's enemy (8)

The expression is: ....

14   Latin to English crossword

The clues are in Latin but your answers should be in English.

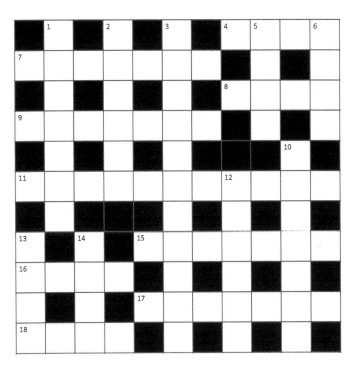

Across

4. Optimum (4)
7. Cogimus (2,5)
8. Videri (4)
9. Occidit (7)
11. Cenamus (2,3,6)
15. Possidebamus (2,5)
16. Id est (2,2)
17. Mansi (1,6)
18. Moritur (4)

Down

1. Recusat (7)
2. Frigidior (6)
3. Perterrita bestia (6,5)
5. Etiam (4)
6. Tempus (4)
10. In febre (2,5)
12. Novum iter (3,3)
13. Mens (4)
14. Cenate (4)

15   English to Latin crossword

The clues are in English but your answers should be in Latin.

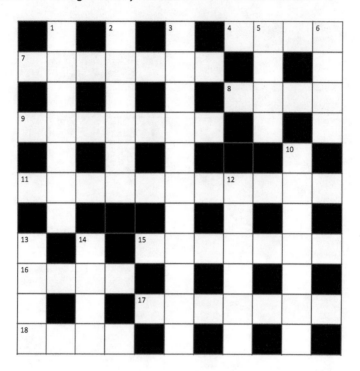

Across

4. Water (4)
7. Noble (7)
8. After (4)
9. You (Pl.) are silent (7)
11. They are faithful (4,7)
15. Of the enemies (7)
16. Kindly woman (4)
17. For the girls (7)
18. Alas (4)

Down

1. A man was called (7)
2. They are afraid (6)
3. A lusty man (11)
5. Those whom (4)
6. Before (4)
10. Money (7)
12. I carried out (6)
13. Such a thing (4)
14. It's all (4)

16   Latin to Latin crossword

The clues are in Latin and your answers should also be in Latin.

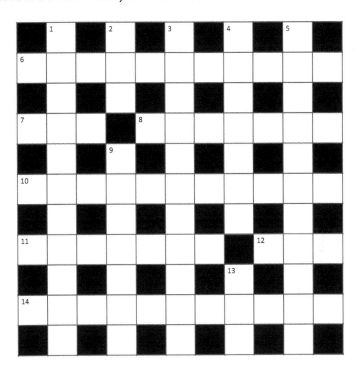

Across

6. Qui exeunt (11)
7. Curo (3)
8. Omnibus diebus (7)
10. Instruentur (11)
11. Ei qui orationem habet (7)
12. Quot? (3)
14. Non ignoro quantum reddere debeam (4,7)

Down

1. Ubi libri continentur (11)
2. Debes scire (3)
3. Sic ingredi (4,7)
4. Signum (7)
5. Haudquaquam tutum (11)
9. Perambulo (7)
13. Sic (3)

17   The Roman way

Solve the riddle by answering all the statements made below. As you answer each question, insert a letter in the grid below, where you will see three words formed.

Word 1

1.   My first is in Cicero and also in Julius.
2.   My second is in Maro and twice in Mamercus.
3.   My third is in Piso and thrice in Poppaea.
4.   My fourth is in Caesar and also in Pompey.
5.   My fifth is in Virgil and also in Horace.
6.   My sixth is in Titus and also in Agricola.
7.   My seventh comes thrice in Augustus and once in Sulla.
8.   My eighth is in Marcus and also in Manlius.

Word 2

1.   My first is in Julius but not in Julia.
2.   My second is in Gaius but not in Gnaeus.
3.   My third is Linus and doubles in Cinna.
4.   My fourth is in Caesar but not in Casca.

Word 3

1.   My first is in Felix and also in Afer.
2.   My second is in Livy and also in Tacitus.
3.   My third is in Agrippina but not in Agrippa.
4.   My fourth is in Cicero but not in Castor.

My whole tells the tale.

1	2	3	4	5	6	7	8

1	2	3	4

1	2	3	4

18 Latin to English crossword

The clues are in Latin but your answers should be in English.

Across

7. Adest omnino facilis (2,4,3,4)
8. Apri (2,4)
9. Simulacra (6)
10. Filius (3)
12. Mittit (5)
14. Et is (3,2)
15. Habet (2,3)
16. Nulla via (2,3)
18. Reges (5)
20. Conari (3)
22. Resolvo (1,5)
23. Hisco (1,5)
24. Sed eam regebamus (3,2,5,3)

Down

1. Quasi is exit (2,2,2,4,3)
2. Ultra (6)
3. Ursae (5)
4. Campus (5)
5. Retinere (6)
6. Hortum video (1,3,3,6)
11. Aliud (5)
13. Modestus (3)
14. Roga (3)
17. Permittit (6)
19. Studeo (1,5)
20. Lacrimae (5)
21. Cedere (5)

19   English to Latin crossword

The clues are in English but your answers should be in Latin.

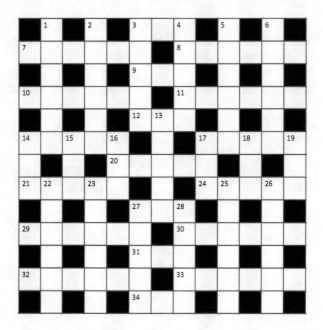

Across

3.   I may be (3)
7.   I received (6)
8.   The last woman (6)
9.   Mouse (3)
10. With a groan (6)
11. Kitchen (6)
12. Her own things (3)
14. Wheel (Acc.) (5)
17. I sent out (5)
20. Outside (5)
21. Inside (5)
24. Actresses (5)
27. Her (3)
29. Shield (6)
30. Unfair things (6)
31. Justice (3)
32. He girded (6)
33. Native inhabitant (6)
34. It is (3)

Down

1.   I approach (6)
2.   Freezing cold things (6)
3.   We may be (5)
4.   A fly (5)
5.   A pen (Acc.) (6)
6.   Of a portent (6)
13. Beyond (5)
14. For the matter (3)
15. So many (3)
16. My things (3)
17. I may go (3)
18. Already (3)
19. Go! (Pl.) (3)
22. Of the night (6)
23. I uncovered (6)
25. I threw in (6)
26. North Wind (6)
27. Buy! (Pl.) (5)
28. She sent (5)

20   Latin to Latin crossword

The clues are in Latin and your answers should also be in Latin.

Across

7. Non abes (4)
8. Consumere (3)
9. Nam (4)
10. Quo tempore? (6)
11. Loculi sine sole (6)
12. Fortasse sum (3)
14. Fatigata (5)
16. Cenae (5)
18. Pulchra (5)
19. Portari (5)
21. Qualis? (5)
23. Devoro (3)
25. Augur (6)
27. Mittis retro (6)
28. Egrediantur (4)
29. Tres casus (3)
30. Discedis   (4)

Down

1. Afferre (8)
2. Quos stultos puto (6)
3. Incolumes (5)
4. Cachinnationem (5)
5. Crura et lacerti (6)
6. Terribilia (4)
13. Id (5)
15. Discedere debes (3)
16. Reddit (3)
17. Hostibus (8)
20. Iterum cogitare debes (6)
22. Contra (6)
23. Morte (5)
24. Precari (5)
26. Solam (4)

21 Abbreviations Wordsearch

Find the abbreviated expressions listed below, which have all been hidden in the grid. Words may go across, backwards, up, down or diagonally. Warning! They have all been written in their full, Latin versions.

A	T	E	T	A	L	I	A	N	O	T	O	N	O	T	A
A	D	R	T	H	N	N	B	N	O	T	A	B	E	N	E
M	E	E	T	S	R	N	E	N	A	D	L	I	B	I	E
E	S	X	R	T	N	N	O	T	A	S	T	E	T	A	R
I	C	I	I	B	I	B	I	D	E	M	S	T	R	R	O
D	T	I	N	N	T	C	R	U	O	R	E	S	L	E	P
I	E	T	R	M	O	R	R	E	T	M	D	A	L	T	M
R	R	R	T	C	E	R	T	I	O	R	I	E	I	E	E
E	S	E	O	L	A	R	G	E	T	M	B	N	B	C	T
M	G	L	T	A	R	R	E	F	N	O	C	S	I	T	O
E	C	A	P	N	I	T	A	C	S	E	I	U	Q	E	R
T	R	E	A	M	U	T	P	I	R	C	S	T	S	O	P
N	A	E	X	E	M	P	L	I	G	R	A	T	I	A	R
A	E	D	E	M	E	I	D	I	R	E	M	T	S	O	P

A.D.	ET AL.	N.B.
A.M.	ETC.	P.M.
C.	IBID.	PRO TEM.
C.F.	I.E.	P.S.
E.G.	LOC. CIT.	R.I.P.

22 Famous Romans: Augustus

See if you can complete the grid below and by so doing, find out the expression which goes down the middle of the grid.

1. The land of Cleopatra (5)
2. Augustus' heir (8)
3. Augustus' wife, mother of 2. (5)
4. Augustus' so-named greater power ..... imperium (5)
5. The battle in western Greece which brought Augustus to power (6)
6. The name of Augustus' tomb, given after a monument in Halicarnassus (9)
7. Augustus' first wife (9)
8. Caesar's one-time Master of Horse, who fled from 5. (6)
9. The name we call him before he became Augustus (8)
10. The orginal name of the month Augustus (8)
11. The woman who could not be named in *nunc est bibendum* (9)
12. The admiral of the winning fleet at 5. (7)
13. Dictator who made Augustus his legal heir (6,6)
14. Augustus is said to have left Rome made of it (6)
15. The man who recruited poets to write for Augustus (8)
16. Augustus's first, given name (5)

The expression is: ....

23   Slowly does it

Try to fit all the Latin words into the grid below. One of them has been done for you, to get you started.

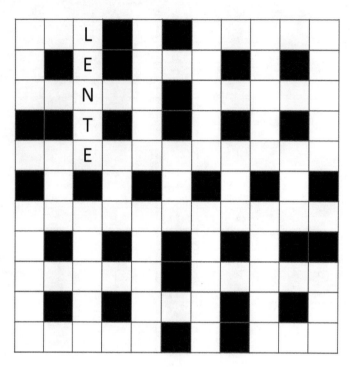

Three letters

EGI
QUO
REI
REX
RUI
SAL
SED
SIM
SIS
TAM
TUA

Five letters

ABEGI
CANTA
CENAE
DENSA
EBRIA
GESSI
GRADU
IUSTE
LECTI
~~LENTE~~
LIMEN

MONES
RANIS
ROGAT
TOGAS
TORSI

Eleven letters

FREQUENTARE
EXCOGITATIS

24   Some things to do

*The object of the puzzle is to find out which letter of the alphabet is represented by each of the 17 numbers used. You are given one word to start you off, so you can begin by entering any letters from this wherever they appear in the grid. Each word you make should be in good Latin. As you decode each letter, write it in the **Letters deciphered** table and cross it off in the **Letters used** table.*

1 Q	2 U	3 A	4 E	5 D	3 A	6 M	■	8	3	6
2	8	■	■	4	■	■	■	17	■	2
4	■	5	9	12	14	3	17	3	13	8
17	■	3	■	9	■	12	■	13	■	3
9	6	14	16	12	9	8	2	12	■	8
■	■	9	■	8	■	17	■	11	■	■
11	■	12	2	4	8	16	13	9	2	12
4	■	3	■	17	■	10	■	15	■	9
7	16	6	6	4	6	16	17	16	■	6
9	■	16	■	■	15	■	■	■	8	2
8	4	17	■	3	10	9	4	13	2	12

Letters deciphered

1	2	3	4	5	6	7	8	9	10	11	12	13	14	15	16	17
Q	U	A	E	D	M											

Letters used

~~A~~	C	~~D~~	~~E~~	F	G	I	L	~~M~~	N	O	P	~~Q~~	R	S	T	~~U~~

25   Latin to English crossword

The clues are in Latin but your answers should be in English.

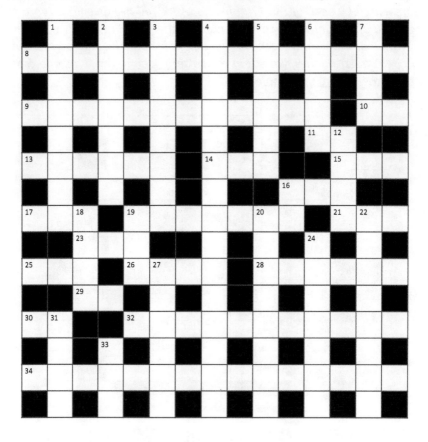

Across

8. Visa es (3,4,4,4)
9. Alienis (3,9)
10. Ad (2)
11. Aut (2)
13. Arsit (6)
14. Vetus (3)
15. Uti (3)
16. Aeger (3)
17. Una (3)
19. Nocte (2,5)
21. Finis (3)
23. Vos (3)
25. Videte (3)
26. Narravit (4)
28. Incipit (6)
29. Tam (2)
30. Super (2)
32. Est in fide (2,2,7)
34. Aperit exta (7,8)

Down

1. Ad columnam (2,6)
2. Agitans (7)
3. Cotidie (5,3)
4. Relinquo in periculo (7,2,6)
5. Detruncare (6)
6. Rogare ita (3,2)
7. Calor (4)
12. Rege (4)
16. Id (2)
18. Oculi (4)
19. Sed (3)
20. Clamat (2,6)
22. Haudquaquam (3,2,3)
24. Erat vir quidam (3,1,3)
27. Gradus (2,4)
31. Proximum (4)
33. Puer (3)

26   English to Latin crossword

The clues are in English but your answers should be in Latin.

Across

8. The men had been surrounded (10,5)
9. Not all of something (4)
10. The avenger (5)
11. Let it stand (4)
12. For a free man (6)
14. I scatter (6)
16. Let me give (3)
18. To make equal (7)
19. Women dispersed (Acc.) (7)
20. Altar (3)
22. Where Octavian and Agrippa met Antony and Cleopatra (6)
24. I cut to pieces (6)
25. For (4)
27. A rare thing (5)
28. Love (4)
29. Senators repeatedly (6,9)

Down

1. He sings cheerfully (9,6)
2. You know (4)
3. I walk (6)
4. To try to catch (7)
5. Of the tiger (6)
6. Tomorrow (4)
7. Among the grander people (5,10)
13. I broke out (5)
15. Rings (5)
16. Goddess (3)
17. My girlfriend (3)
21. To return (7)
23. Grumpily (6)
24. They pick up (6)
26. Death (4)
28. She leaves (4)

27 Latin to Latin crossword

The clues are in Latin and your answers should also be in Latin.

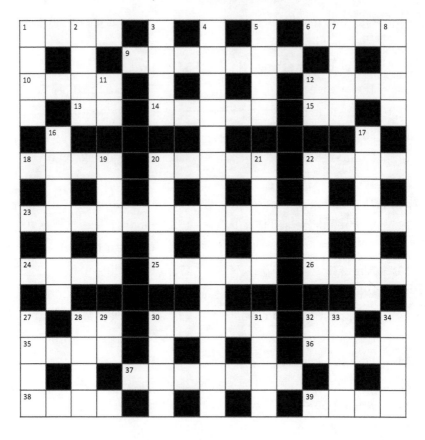

Across

1.	Intra septem et novem (4)
6.	Consumit (4)
9.	Instrue (7)
10.	Non mala (4)
12.	Vobis singulariter (4)
13.	Atque (2)
14.	Sine mente (5)
15.	Estis singulariter (2)
18.	In sella manere debes (4)
20.	Frigori oppositum (5)
22.	In casa alicuius (4)
23.	Eis qui circumstant (15)
24.	Carmen facio (4)
25.	Multis occasionibus (5)
26.	Familiaribus ipsius (4)
28.	Ille (2)
30.	Nosco (5)
32.	Non ad (2)
35.	Ille infamis (4)
36.	Reddant (4)
37.	Factum velut equus Troiae (7)
38.	Illi non alii (4)
39.	Quod cum libro facio (4)

Down

1.	Sphaera (4)
2.	Habe (4)
3.	Ora! (4)
4.	Fortasse vocati erant (9,6)
5.	Pondus (4)
7.	Divis (4)
8.	Amicis tui (4)
11.	Sed (2)
12.	Vos singulariter (2)
16.	Didonem (7)
17.	Amoenitas (7)
19.	Expello (5)
20.	Amicus (5)
21.	Qui coracinant (5)
22.	Non idem (5)
27.	Luci (4)
28.	Is cum aliis (4)
29.	Quem in speculo videt (2)
30.	Tum (4)
31.	Labor (4)
32.	Non ab (2)
33.	Commode (4)
34.	Piceo (4)

28   A Roman whodunnit

See if you can solve the riddle.

Mortuus est imperator, sed quis eum necavit?

Augustus, gladio servi sui vulneratus, in regno Plutonis nunc habitat.
Re vera, percussor erat unus e tribus servis, atque tibi necesse est eum invenire.
Caelius fortasse dominum interfecit, quod ille suum patrem in servitudinem traxisset, qui priusquam tabernarius in urbe Londinio fuerat.
Utrum Lurcio, cuius sororem Augustus in Galliam miserat, postquam ea dixit imperatorem asino similem esse, an Marcus eum necaverit, cui imperator semper crediderat sed semper ei odio erat?
Sed tu, quid putas?

Specta primum, deinde invenire poteris.

Percussor erat: ....

29   It's difficult

*The object of the puzzle is to find out which letter of the alphabet is represented by each of the 16 numbers used. You are given one word to start you off, so you can begin by entering any letters from this wherever they appear in the grid. Each word you make should be in good Latin. As you decode each letter, write it in the **Letters deciphered** table and cross it off in the **Letters used** table.*

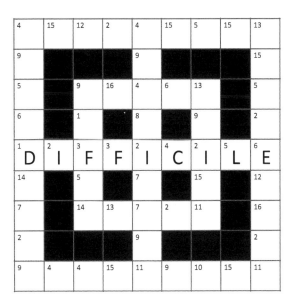

Letters deciphered

1	2	3	4	5	6	7	8	9	10	11	12	13	14	15	16
D	I	F	C	L	E										

Letters used

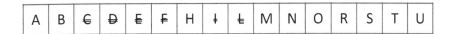

A	B	C̶	D̶	E̶	F̶	H	I̶	L̶	M	N	O	R	S	T	U

33

30 Latin to English crossword

The clues are in Latin but your answers should be in English.

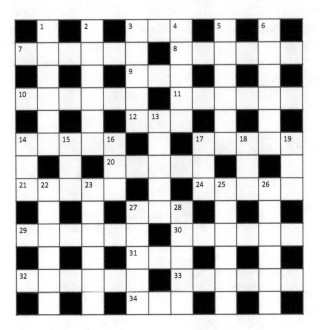

Across

3. Pone (3)
7. Volumen (6)
8. Constat (6)
9. Robur (3)
10. Probus (6)
11. Expellit (6)
12. Nefas (3)
14. Non est (2,3)
17. Peritus (5)
20. Accuratus (5)
21. Lingua Romanorum (5)
24. Hostis (5)
27. Vetus (3)
29. Ludus (6)
30. Ingreditur (6)
31. Fragor (3)
32. Rarus (6)
33. Cantor (6)
34. Rem graviter ferre (3)

Down

1. Trans (6)
2. Advenire (4,2)
3. Coniurat (5)
4. Captum (5)
5. Comes (6)
6. Prohibemus (2,4)
13. Omnino (2,3)
14. Aeger (3)
15. Rete (3)
16. Decem (3)
17. Consumpsit (3)
18. Oculus (3)
19. Conari (3)
22. Recipere (6)
23. Lugeo (1,5)
25. Memorans (6)
26. Mercatus (6)
27. Senior (5)
28. Creber (5)

31   English to Latin crossword

The clues are in English but your answers should be in Latin.

Across

7. Water (4)
8. Hello (3)
9. I have been away (4)
10. Countryside (3)
11. Not (3)
12. Of a man (4)
13. Come on! (Sing.) (3)
15. It will be (4)
18. A lesser man (5)
20. To rush (5)
22. A short thing (5)
23. To be able to (5)
25. A greater woman (5)
27. That awful woman (4)
29. Buy! (Sing.) (3)
31. Other things (4)
32. Why (3)
33. But (3)
34. To give (4)
35. The matter (3)
36. I say (4)

Down

1. For a cavalryman (6)
2. Few men (4)
3. House (4)
4. Well (4)
5. Plainly (4)
6. A harder man (6)
14. I was wearing (7)
16. The city (Acc.) (5)
17. Press! (Sing.) (5)
19. We (3)
21. Get out! (Sing.) (3)
24. You're standing in the way (6)
26. I objected (6)
28. Sharp man (4)
29. I wander (4)
30. To be (4)
31. I add (4)

32   Latin to Latin crossword

The clues are in Latin and your answers should also be in Latin.

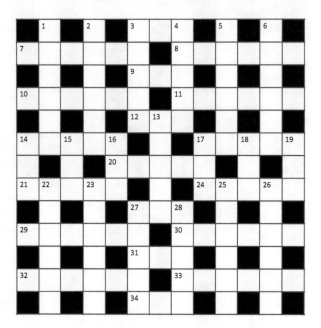

Across

3. Ego tecum (3)
7. Regredior (6)
8. Assigna (6)
9. Aegre (3)
10. Fidum (6)
11. Nescio (6)
12. Id quod solet (3)
14. Audax es (5)
17. Urgeo (5)
20. Quocum pluit (5)
21. Silet (5)
24. Altissima (5)
27. Adora (3)
29. Superabo (6)
30. In equum conscendo (6)
31. Vivit (3)
32. Fortasse (6)
33. Acerbe (6)
34. Tibi esse licet (3)

Down

1. Regressu (6)
2. Quaerere (6)
3. Tres triplex (5)
4. Rupibus (5)
5. Arbitror (6)
6. Caverna (6)
13. Sphaeram (5)
14. Vel (3)
15. Praesta (3)
16. Forsitan est (3)
17. Finis cruris (3)
18. Illam (3)
19. Roga! (3)
22. Eos qui omnia cupiunt (6)
23. Absolvo (6)
25. Usu rapio (6)
26. Variare (6)
27. Insanus (5)
28. Tempus vitae (5)

33   Sudoku

You know how Sudoku works. All you have to do is to place numbers one to nine in each vertical and horizontal line and then make sure that each number appears once in each of the nine 3x3 squares. The difference here is that this is Roman Sudoku!

You use the numbers as below:

1	2	3	4	5	6	7	8	9
I	II	III	IV	V	VI	VII	VIII	IX

	III	VI	V	IX			I	VIII
IX				III		IV	VII	
IV	II	V			VIII			
				VI	III		IX	
I		IX		II		VI		VII
II			IX	VII				
		II	I			V		VI
	I	VIII		IV				III
	VII			V	II		VIII	

34   Famous Romans: Nero

See if you can complete the grid below and by so doing, find out the expression which goes down the middle of the grid.

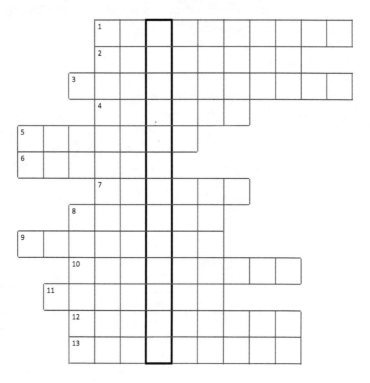

1.   The Golden House (5,5)
2.   Nero's stepfather (8)
3.   Nero's stepbrother (11)
4.   The tutor who was also the praetorian prefect (6)
5.   She was married to Otho before becoming Nero's second wife (7)
6.   Where Nero was born (6)
7.   The person who started the rebellion against Nero in France (6)
8.   The tutor who was also the philosopher (6)
9.   The British queen who rebelled (8)
10.   The disaster in Rome which people said Nero caused (5,4)
11.   Nero's first wife (7)
12.   Nero's mother (9)
13.   Nero's biographer (9)

The expression is: ....

35 Unwanted

The object of the puzzle is to find out which letter of the alphabet is represented by each of the 18 numbers used. You are given one word to start you off, so you can begin by entering any letters from this wherever they appear in the grid. Each word you make should be in good Latin. As you decode each letter, write it in the __Letters deciphered__ table and cross it off in the __Letters used__ table.

	12		12		14		13	11		5
1 N	2 O	3 L	4 E	5 B	6 A	1 N	7 T		17	4
	13		16		5		6	7		1
4	13	7		18	11	13			13	4
	15		8		7		1		7	
6	17	5	15	3	6	5	6	17	15	13
	15		2		18		17		3	
4	13			4	11	13		11	7	6
10		7	15		13				11	
11	1		1	11	7	11	9	11	2	16
7		9	6		11		2		16	

Letters deciphered

1	2	3	4	5	6	7	8	9	10	11	12	13	14	15	16	17	18
N	O	L	E	B	A	T											

Letters used

A	B	D	E	H	I	L	M	N	O	P	Q	R	S	T	U	V	X

36   Latin to English crossword

The clues are in Latin but your answers should be in English.

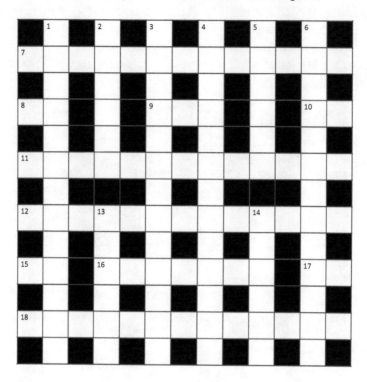

Across

7. Ubi erant? (5,4,4)
8. Apud (2)
9. Devora (3)
10. Nos (2)
11. Conveniebamus (2,4,7)
12. Inimici milites (5,8)
15. Id (2)
16. Scaena (7)
17. Sursum (2)
18. Lasse iter facere (6,7)

Down

1. Natura mutata (7,6)
2. Aura (6)
3. Dulciores odores (7,6)
4. Scripta epistula (7,6)
5. tandem (2,4)
6. Superbe redire (6,7)
13. Causa (6)
14. In auribus (2,4)

37   English to Latin crossword

The clues are in English but your answers should be in Latin.

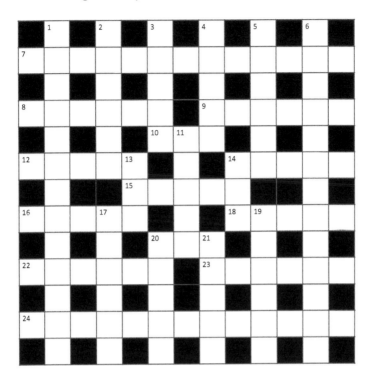

Across

7. The women had been brought together (8,5)
8. I turn away (6)
9. He will choose (6)
10. You may be (3)
12. I may know (5)
14. Things moved out (5)
15. Also (5)
16. Greedy woman (5)
18. I ordered (5)
20. Love! (3)
22. Donkey (6)
23. A short man (6)
24. Along the hard road (3,4,6)

Down

1. She might have called together (13)
2. Renown (6)
3. and 4. Black cats (Acc.) (5,5)
5. Of cities (6)
6. A most huge lady (Acc.) (13)
11. Troy (5)
13. My things (3)
14. I bought (3)
17. I renew (6)
19. By burning (6)
20. Province around Troy (Acc.) (5)
21. Let me go away (5)

38   Latin to Latin crossword

The clues are in Latin and your answers should also be in Latin.

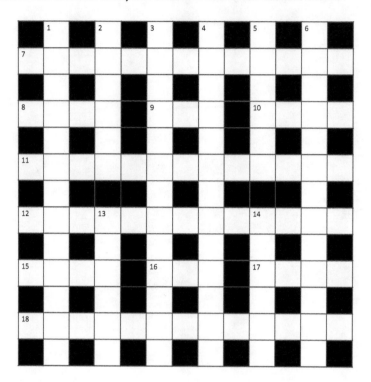

Across

7. Tituli (13)
8. Trusi (4)
9. Ad quem (3)
10. Litora (4)
11. Intrabat (13)
12. Locus spectaculorum (13)
15. Addere debes (4)
16. Quare (3)
17. Contendes (4)
18. Compositum intellexi (8,5)

Down

1. Ingrediuntur doctores (7,6)
2. Acutior (6)
3. Abi tranquille (7,6)
4. Conservare principia (8,5)
5. Femina non laeta (6)
6. Quem ut dicunt, cenabit (9,4)
13. Tempestatis (6)
14. Consterno (6)

39   A Roman riddle

See if you can solve the riddle. If you do, you will know how to reward yourself!

Magister aliquid celare conatur, quod tibi necesse est invenire.

Multis vestigiis huius inquisitionis sepultis in hac fabula, tibi litterae inveniendae sunt quae in lingua Britannorum unum verbum faciant; tum huic taberna addenda est. His duobus verbis a te cognitis scriptisque in hac cera, tibi indulgere possis!

Vestigium primum est littera prima huius operis, deinde littera prima omnium. Aliud inveniendum est in medio cerae. Finis tandem ultimum est vestigium quartum. Omne est. Sed quid est praemium? Si cognoveris, tibi hoc habeas!

Praemium tibi est: ....

40   Latin to English crossword

The clues are in Latin but your answers should be in English.

Across

1. Colles (5)
4. Rursus (5)
7. Nos (2)
8. Ad (2)
9. Gratias egit (7)
11. Rursus designavit (11)
12. Roga salutationem (3,8)
14. Linguae (7)
15. Minime! (2)
17. Ut (2)
18. Delabitur (5)
19. Nidi (5)

Down

1. Ingentior (5)
2. Est (2)
3. Turba fert (5,6)
4. In vicem reposcere (3,2,6)
5. Id (2)
6. Memoravit (5)
9. Hac nocte (7)
10. Retinet (7)
12. Saltus (5)
13. Gramen (5)
16. Aut (2)
17. Apud (2)

41   English to Latin crossword

The clues are in English but your answers should be in Latin.

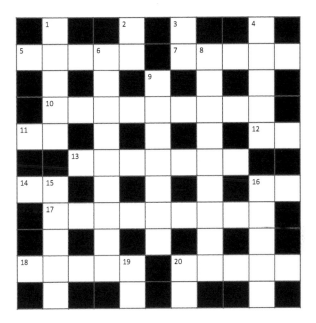

Across

5.   Men who don't drink (5)
7.   With you (5)
10. I summoned (9)
11. First person object (2)
12. Away from (2)
13. Mix it all up! (Pl.) (7)
14. Second person subject (2)
16. Towards (2)
17. Rude people (9)
18. By far (5)
20. I despise (5)

Down

1.   She-bears (5)
2.   To him (2)
3.   Even (2)
4.   Senate House (5)
6.   They have been led (5,4)
8.   Letters (9)
9.   She's a dear (3,4)
15. All the time (5)
16. Donkeys (5)
19. On account of (2)
20. Second person object (2)

42   Latin to Latin crossword

The clues are in Latin and your answers should also be in Latin.

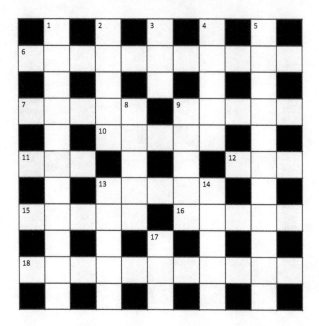

Across

6. Cuius signum est cornucopia (11)
7. Velut (5)
9. Pura (5)
10. Incolumem (5)
11. At (3)
12. Vivit (3)
13. Cupiam (5)
15. Noveris (5)
16. Nec nimium nec parum (5)
18. Magistrum litterarum (11)

Down

1. Gradatim tacere (11)
2. Non extra est (5)
3. Adeo (3)
4. Quoque (5)
5. Eum qui maxime gaudeat (11)
8. Imperas (5)
9. Desideras (5)
13. Eheu mihi (3,2)
14. Amplius (5)
17. Aequalis (3)

43　　Let it come

*The object of the puzzle is to find out which letter of the alphabet is represented by each of the 18 numbers used. You are given one word to start you off, so you can begin by entering any letters from this wherever they appear in the grid. Each word you make should be in good Latin. As you decode each letter, write it in the **Letters deciphered** table and cross it off in the **Letters used** table.*

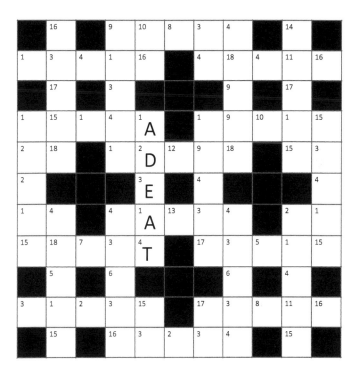

Letters deciphered

1	2	3	4	5	6	7	8	9	10	11	12	13	14	15	16	17	18
A	D	E	T														

Letters used

A	B	C	D̶	E̶	F	G	I	L	M	N	O	P	R	S	T̶	U	V

47

44   Famous Romans: Hadrian

See if you can complete the grid below and by so doing, find out the expression which goes down the middle of the grid.

1.   Hadrian's main guardian (6)
2.   The wife of 1. who helped Hadrian become emperor (7)
3.   Hadrian's heir, later called Pius (9)
4.   Hadrian's mother-in-law (7)
5.   Hadrian's family name (6)
6.   Hadrian's home town in Spain (7)
7.   The temple to all gods in Rome, designed by Hadrian (7)
8.   The location of the famous Hadrian's villa (6)
9.   Hadrian's wife (6)
10.   The title of the Empress (7)
11.   Hadrian's young male companion (8)
12.   The name of Hadrian's frontier system in Germany (5)
13.   A city where Hadrian became Archon (6)

The expression is: ....

45   Latin to English crossword

The clues are in Latin but your answers should be in English.

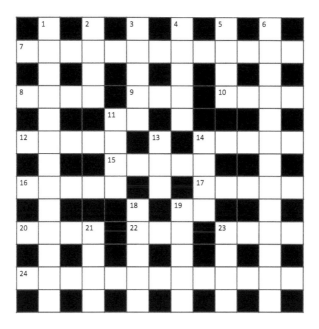

Across

7. Altera sententia (6,7)
8. Moritur (4)
9. Poema (3)
10. Oppidum (4)
11. Illud (2)
12. Numquam (5)
14. Avunculus (5)
15. Aperit (5)
16. Septem (5)
17. Ulna (5)
19. Nos (2)
20. Eheu (4)
22. Cucurrit (3)
23. Rates (4)
24. Duae novae legiones (3,3,7)

Down

1. Attulit leges (9,4)
2. Digiti (4)
3. Fatuus quidam (5)
4. Fur (5)
5. Pulvis (4)
6. Illa offendet (3,4,6)
11. Ferrum (4)
13. Novus (3)
14. Consumit (4)
18. Turba (5)
19. Sub (5)
21. Mitte (4)
23. Clades (4)

46 English to Latin crossword

The clues are in English but your answers should be in Latin.

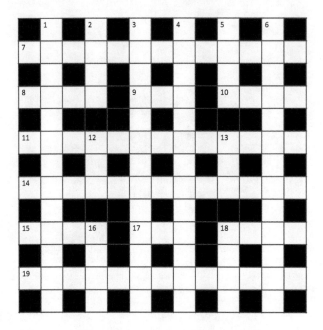

Across

7. Of the epitaph (13)
8. Family (4)
9. Heart (3)
10. It goes out (4)
11. Building work applied (4,9)
14. It was broken so I am cutting it out (7,6)
15. For (4)
17. I hurry (3)
18. A few things (4)
19. He's difficult through and through (13)

Down

1. Out of control (13)
2. You (Sing.) know (4)
3. Rufus' divorce (9,4)
4. Cicero's journey (4,9)
5. To be about to be (4)
6. A very small man runs (7,6)
12. Thus (3)
13. Justice (3)
16. Only (4)
18. For the defendants (4)

47   Latin to Latin crossword

The clues are in Latin and your answers should also be in Latin.

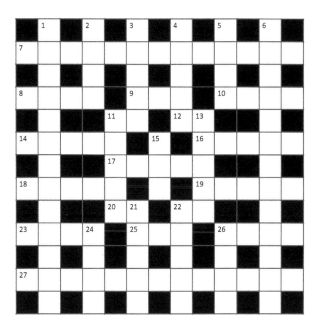

Across

7. Non potes celerius ire! (4,9)
8. Debes bibere! (4)
9. Cessit (3)
10. Maneat (4)
11. Illa (2)
12. Sed (2)
14. Volumen (5)
16. Quoque (5)
17. Exercitus in motu (5)
18. Otium (5)
19. Luctus (5)
20. Ille (2)
22. Confero (2)
23. Sumpsi (4)
25. Detestor (3)
26. Divitiae (4)
27. Construxeram (13)

Down

1. Desertor, vae! (9,4)
2. Totum (4)
3. Aula (5)
4. Quae est intra quintam et septimam (5)
5. Civitas (4)
6. Princeps versabatur (9,4)
11. Abolevi (5)
13. Produco (5)
15. Diligo (3)
21. Amici (5)
22. Deae (5)
24. Ingrediris (4)
26. Prodigium (4)

48   Latin to English crossword

The clues are in Latin but your answers should be in English.

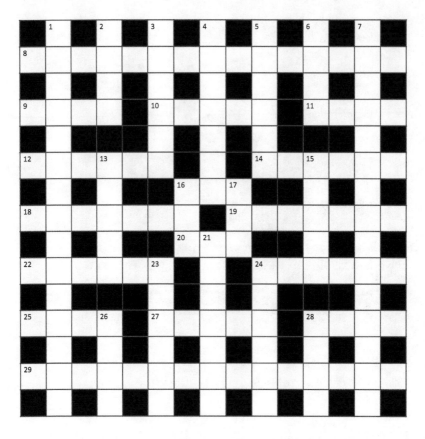

Across

8. Pulcherrime (4,11)
9. Prohibe (4)
10. Fossa (5)
11. Dicit (4)
12. Praedium (6)
14. Solus (6)
16. Ac (3)
18. Improbus (7)
19. Meliorare (7)
20. Crus (3)
22. Recuso (6)
24. Hastae (6)
25. Terra (4)
27. Viae (5)
28. Trahe! (4)
29. Coactum est (2,3,4,6)

Down

1. Foedae bestiae (9,6)
2. In summo (4)
3. Acus (6)
4. Sustine (7)
5. Pugnat (6)
6. Soles (4)
7. Ludere callida (4,6,5)
13. Surrexit (5)
15. Nutrix (5)
16. Omnis (3)
17. Fodere (3)
21. Fugit (7)
23. Palpitat (6)
24. Adeo tener (2,4)
26. Surda (4)
28. Aude (4)

49   English to Latin crossword

The clues are in English but your answers should be in Latin.

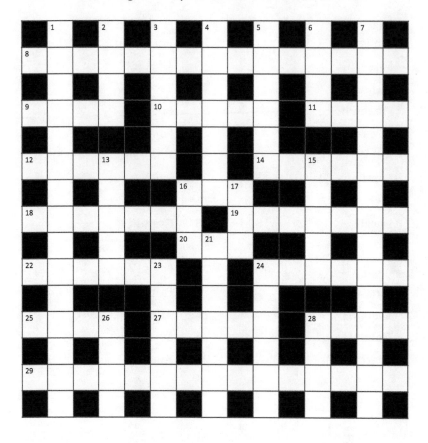

Across

8. They had been unpunished (8,7)
9. River bank (4)
10. You are quiet (5)
11. Three (4)
12. Bring up! (6)
14. At once (6)
16. Bronze (3)
18. To address (7)
19. I went in (7)
20. So (3)
22. To be written (6)
24. I sow (6)
25. Then (4)
27. Blind woman (5)
28. I conquered (4)
29. I go forward rightly (5,10)

Down

1. It's to be said to all (7,8)
2. Concern (4)
3. A consul's attendant (6)
4. To gape (7)
5. Race (6)
6. It will be (4)
7. Amongst the men lined up (5,10)
13. For a flower (5)
15. Out of his wits (5)
16. She says (3)
17. Let me be (3)
21. Foreigners (Acc.) (7)
23. I began (6)
24. On the breeze (2,4)
26. Entrails (4)
28. I saw (4)

50 Latin to Latin crossword

The clues are in Latin and your answers should also be in Latin.

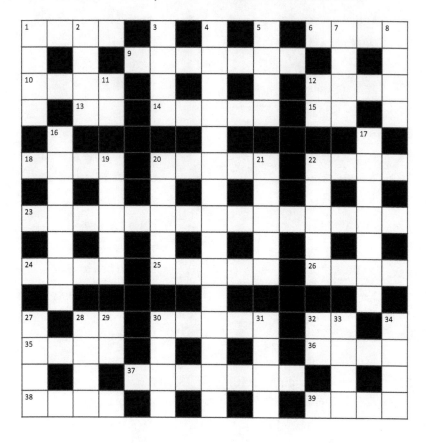

Across

1. Quod viam trans fluvium ducit (4)
6. Egi (4)
9. Perturbata (7)
10. Recentia (4)
12. Illius (4)
13. Hoc (2)
14. Metallum flavum (5)
15. Vultus (2)
18. In tempore vetere (4)
20. Sphaerae (5)
22. Sagax (4)
23. Ascensores non sine quadrupedibus (7,3,5)
24. Lux (4)
25. Auricula (5)
26. Totum (4)
28. Num (2)
30. Etiam nunc (5)
32. Contra (2)
35. Quae mellificant (4)
36. Frico (4)
37. Circumdant (7)
38. Haudquaquam abes (4)
39. Preces (4)

Down

1. Loca! (4)
2. Scio (4)
3. Vestis senatoria (4)
4. Urbs scelesta quae Romam minata erat (7,8)
5. Eodem modo (4)
7. Discedis (4)
8. Illa femina, non alia (4)
11. Non ab (2)
12. Ibi (2)
16. Quodpiam (7)
17. Comiter (7)
19. Amplius (5)
20. Labores (5)
21. Vivimus (5)
22. Comparo (5)
27. Rumor (4)
28. Illi reflexi duplicatique (4)
29. Ille (2)
30. Aggreditur (4)
31. Carmen facio (4)
32. Vadit (2)
33. Occido (4)
34. Appella! (4)

51   Diamond words

Insert your answers into the diamond-shaped grid below, which should all be single words in Latin. You may notice that all the letters of the shorter words become anagrams of the longer ones above or below them, along with one more letter, which should make life quite easy for you. Good luck.

1.   Soldier (Abbrev.)

2.   My

3.   I may be

4.   You (Sing.) buy

5.   Sad

6.   You (Sing.) tremble

7.   She had sent

8.   Teacher

9.   You (Pl.) may rule

10. You (Sing.) repeat

11. To stand

12. You (Sing.) were

13. Things

14. Themselves

15. Out of

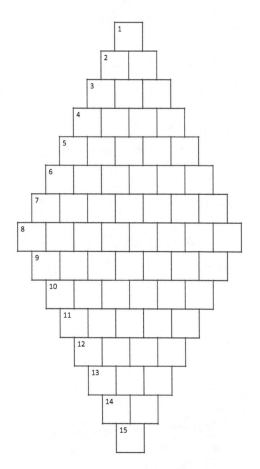

52   Diamond words

Insert your answers into the diamond-shaped grid below, which should all be single words in Latin. You may notice that all the letters of the shorter words become anagrams of the longer ones above or below them, along with one more letter, which should make life quite easy for you. Good luck.

1. By

2. Those things

3. Alas

4. Chester

5. I escape

6. Eat! (Sing.)

7. I turn to

8. One who leaves the path

9. Originates from

10. To be forbidden

11. I have turned

12. Of the truth

13. Man

14. By force

15. Five

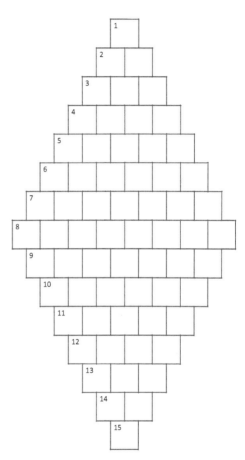

53   Diamond words

Insert your answers into the diamond-shaped grid below, which should all be single words in Latin. You may notice that all the letters of the shorter words become anagrams of the longer ones above or below them, along with one more letter, which should make life quite easy for you. Good luck.

1.   Out of

2.   Myself

3.   I buy

4.   Pole

5.   I fear

6.   In the best way

7.   I obtain a request

8.   She may beg

9.   For the time

10.   He presses

11.   It dies

12.   Ceremonially

13.   To go

14.   Those men

15.   Go! (Sing.)

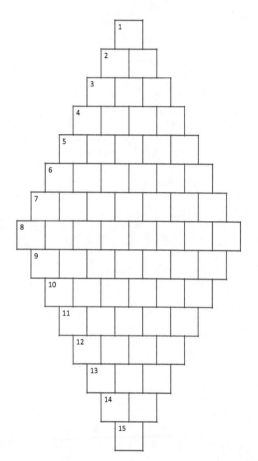

54   Six all round

Look carefully at the grid below. Your job is to write your answers to the clues around the numbers, always beginning in the cell space immediately above the number. The answers are all six letter words in Latin but the difficulty for you is that some go clockwise around the number and some go anti-clockwise. Good luck in working out which is which.

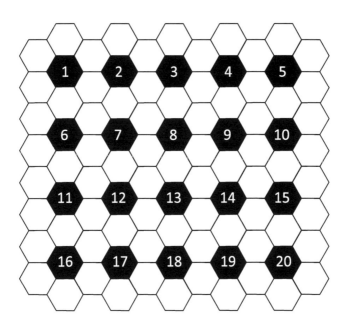

1.	Enemy	11.	To urge
2.	Ditches	12.	To warn
3.	Poets	13.	Mountains
4.	I am stunned	14.	Deaths
5.	Studies	15.	North wind
6.	Burial mounds	16.	I put out
7.	Highest	17.	Seek out! (Sing.)
8.	Three years old	18.	Sadly
9.	First man	19.	For three
10.	For two	20.	Departure

55 Six all round

Look carefully at the grid below. Your job is to write your answers to the clues around the numbers, always beginning in the cell space immediately above the number. The answers are all six letter words in Latin but the difficulty for you is that some go clockwise around the number and some go anti-clockwise. Good luck in working out which is which.

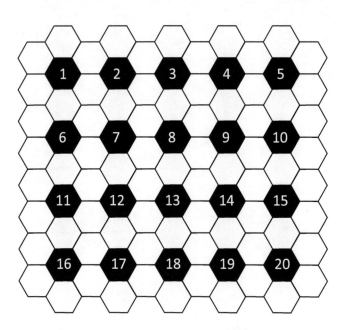

1. Indeed	11. I feast
2. At last	12. Banquet
3. Kitchen	13. Seats
4. Worshipper	14. War
5. I speak forth	15. Command
6. To lead	16. Abundant
7. To say	17. Shores
8. To be angry	18. I take to court
9. Beam of wood	19. Soft down
10. Face	20. Gore

56   Six all round

Look carefully at the grid below. Your job is to write your answers to the clues around the numbers, always beginning in the cell space immediately above the number. The answers are all six letter words in Latin but the difficulty for you is that some go clockwise around the number and some go anti-clockwise. Good luck in working out which is which.

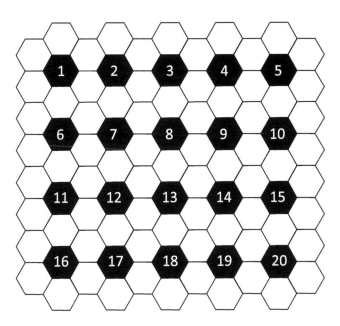

1.	Savage	11.	You (Sing.) swim over
2.	Soft shoe	12.	She hands over
3.	I will hurt	13.	He presses
4.	I will be quiet	14.	Stomach
5.	Old-fashioned lady	15.	Thick
6.	Courage	16.	To shine
7.	Chaste	17.	To grieve
8.	Things which slipped by	18.	Soft men
9.	Washes away	19.	You (Sing.) will lift
10.	Running tracks	20.	Usual things

57 Double trouble - expose envy

Put your answers in English to the clues which are in Latin in the grids below. You may have one problem, however: there are two questions for each of the clues and you have to decide into which grid the right answers should go. Two words have been given to start you off. Bonam fortunam.

Grid 1 (with "EXPOSE" filled at 8 across)

Grid 2 (with "ENVY" filled at 18 across)

ACROSS

3. Quid (4) **** Sella (4)
6. Iugulum (6) **** Quartus (6)
7. Minime (2) **** Meus (2)
8. Expono (6) **** Dolor (6)
10. Est (2) **** Apud (2)
11. Ut (2) **** Esto (2)
12. Memoria (6) **** Fides (6)
15. Nos (2) **** Ite (2)
17. Dux (6) **** Aperte (6)
18. Oppidum (4) **** Invidia (4)

DOWN

1. Dono (6) **** Eligo (6)
2. Vota (4) **** Arbor (4)
3. Flagellum (4) **** Stella (4)
4. Sum (2) **** Quidam (2)
5. Formae (5) **** Debere (2,3)
9. Obtemperavit (6) **** Tuto (6)
10. Simulacrum (5) **** De (5)
13. Solum (4) **** Ferrum (4)
14. Annus (4) **** Effugiebat (4)
16. In (2) **** Ita (2)

58   Double trouble - sicut senatores

Put your answers in Latin to the clues which are in English in the grids below. You may have one problem, however: there are two questions for each of the clues and you have to decide into which grid the right answers should go. Two words have been given to start you off. Bonam fortunam.

ACROSS

5.	About to prepare (9) **** ~~Senators~~ (9)
6.	Pig (3) **** Go to! (Sing.) (3)
8.	~~Just as~~ (5) **** School (5)
9.	For God (3) **** You (Sing.) may give (3)
10.	I limit (5) **** Another thing (5)
11.	He says (3) **** I stand (3)
13.	To break into (9) **** Five hundred (9)

DOWN

1.	Egyptian goddess (4) **** Suitable things (4)
2.	I rooted out (4) **** Burden (4)
3.	A good man (5) **** I hear (5)
4.	Piles (6) **** They cover (6)
7.	Everywhere (6) **** To destroy (6)
8.	Lion (3) **** But (3)
9.	A hard thing (5) **** Worthy men (5)
11.	They are (4) **** Bees (4)
12.	Three (4) **** She goes to meet (4)

59   Double trouble - asper editor

Put your answers in Latin to the clues which are also in Latin in the grids below. You may have one problem, however: there are two questions for each of the clues and you have to decide into which grid the right answers should go. Two words have been given to start you off. Bonam fortunam.

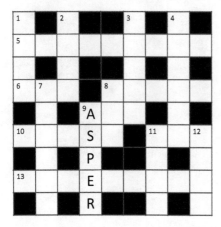

ACROSS

5. Complere (9) **** Copiosiores (9)
6. Brevi tempore (3) **** Factum (3)
8. Ianua (5) **** Fierem (5)
9. Quod ego facio, factum est ... (1,2) **** Trans (3)
10. Horribilis (5) **** Effugi (5)
11. Calliditas (3) **** Sancta (3)
13. Mortalibus (9) **** Vicit (9)

DOWN

1. Acutus (4) **** Furtim (4)
2. Pecus (4) **** Solus (4)
3. Potestatem habere (5) **** Qui fabulam in scaena agit (5)
4. Consanguineus (6) **** Candidi (6)
7. ~~Is qui edit~~ (6) **** Is qui obviam it (6)
8. Quod cruris in fine est (3) **** Mercatus sum (3)
9. ~~Crassus~~ (5) **** Castigo (5)
11. Duo (4) **** Avis Iunonis (4)
12. Ipsos (4) **** Sublime (4)

60   Home for prayers

Below you will find two grids and a set of double clues. Your job is to put the right answers in the right boxes of the right grids. You may notice that all the letters of the shorter words go into the longer ones above or below them along with one more letter, which should make life quite easy for you. Good luck.

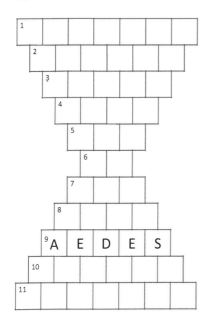 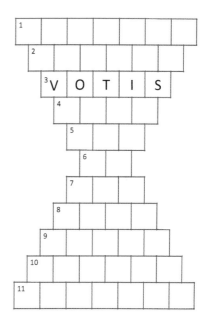

1. You (Pl.) know (7) *** You (Pl.) might give (7)
2. You (Sing.) will hand over (6) *** I visit (6)
3. ~~For prayers~~ (5) *** He calms down (5)
4. You (Sing.) are present (4) *** Sheep (4)
5. You (Sing.) want (3) *** Goddess (3)
6. About (2) *** He (2)
7. Of themselves (3) *** But (3)
8. You (Sing.) may give out (4) *** You (Sing.) rush (4)
9. ~~Home~~ (5) *** Earlier (5)
10. You (Sing.) may return (6) *** First (6)
11. Abandoned things (7) *** You (Sing.) break out (7)

61   Fools to dance

Below you will find two grids and a set of double clues. Your job is to put the right answers in the right boxes of the right grids. You may notice that all the letters of the shorter words go into the longer ones above or below them along with one more letter, which should make life quite easy for you. Good luck.

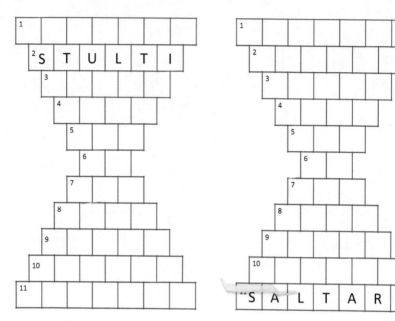

1.   You (Pl.) carried (7) *** Straight things (7)
2.   She might go to (6) *** ~~Fools~~ (6)
3.   Shore (5) *** Nets (5)
4.   On a raft (4) *** In place (4)
5.   Three times (3) *** To use (3)
6.   So that (2) *** And (2)
7.   Let him go (3) *** Or (3)
8.   She may rush (4) *** Such a thing (4)
9.   Another (5) *** Bulls (5)
10. Things carried back (6) *** Main hall (6)
11. ~~To dance~~ (7) *** It chews over (7)

68

62   Poor rotter

Below you will find two grids and a set of double clues. Your job is to put the right answers in the right boxes of the right grids. You may notice that all the letters of the shorter words go into the longer ones above or below them along with one more letter, which should make life quite easy for you. Good luck.

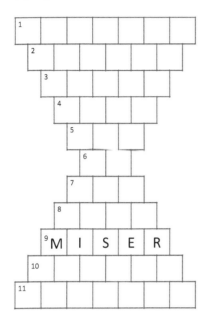 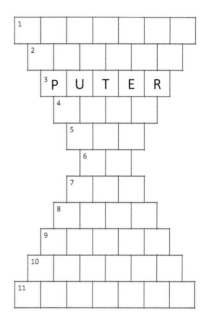

    1.   To exult (7) *** He overpowers (7)

    2.   Think back! (Sing.) (6) *** Big cats (6)

    3.   ~~Rotten man~~ (5) *** You (Sing.) rule (5)

    4.   To be worn (4) *** On a rock (4)

    5.   I acted (3) *** Through (3)

    6.   They (2) *** In fact (2)

    7.   By mouth (3) *** To go (3)

    8.   Oars (4) *** I wander (4)

    9.   ~~Poor~~ (5) *** I may delay (5)

    10.   With a rumour (6) *** I sent back (6)

    11.   Granary (7) *** In laps (7)

63   Arrowword

All the clues are on the grid and the answers should all be in Latin.

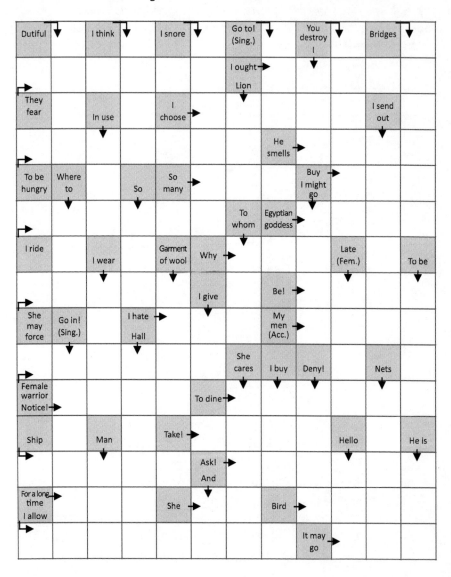

64   Arrowword

All the clues are on the grid and the answers should all be in Latin.

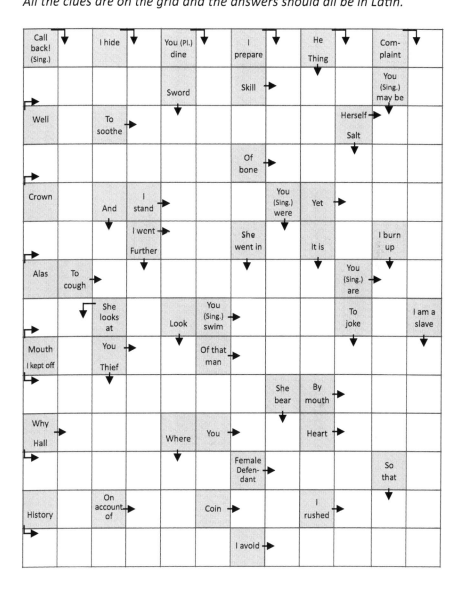

65   Arrowword

All the clues are on the grid and the answers should all be in Latin.

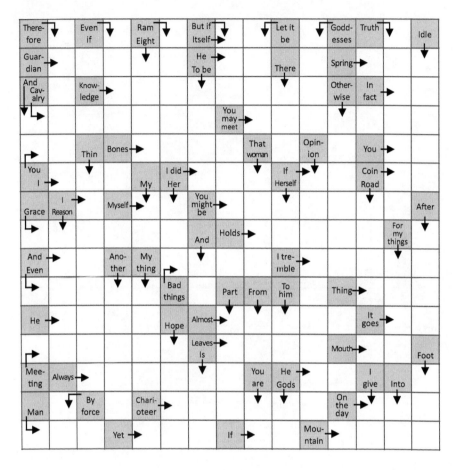

Solutions

1 Latin to English crossword

2 English to Latin crossword

3 Latin to Latin crossword

4 Famous Romans: Aeneas

The answer: HIC LABOR EST
(This famous line comes from Virgil's Aeneid VI.129)

5 Latin phrases wordsearch

	S						I			I	O
I	T				A	N			N	T	
D	A	D	H	O	C	R	P		V	C	
N	T		P	A	X	E	E		I	A	
A	U	N	E		S	T	R		N	F	
R	S	O	R		I	E	P		I	O	E
E	Q	N	A		V	C	E	N	N	V	D
P	U	A	N		A	T	T		T	E	
O	O	U	N		A	E	U		E	R	
S		Q	U		R		U		R	I	
U		E	M	A	A		M		I	T	
D		N	L		R			M	A		
O		I	T	E	R	M	I	N	U	S	
M	A	S	A	D	N	A	U	S	E	A	M

6 Sudoku

III	V	VII	II	VI	VIII	IV	IX	I
IV	VI	IX	I	III	V	II	VII	VIII
I	II	VIII	VII	IX	IV	V	III	VI
V	VIII	IV	III	VII	I	VI	II	IX
VII	IX	I	VI	V	II	VIII	IV	III
II	III	VI	VIII	IV	IX	VII	I	V
VI	I	V	IX	II	VII	III	VIII	IV
IX	VII	III	IV	VIII	VI	I	V	II
VIII	IV	II	V	I	III	IX	VI	VII

7 With love, the end

G	A	L	E	A		C	U	R	A	T
E		A	M		E		A		R	
N	A	R	R	O		S	U	M	M	A
U		G		R	E	S		I		X
S	T	A	R	E		I	U	S	S	I
			E			T				
P	A	L	M	A		F	I	N	E	S
E		A		M	E	I		O		C
C	A	P	R	A		N	O	C	T	U
U		I		R		I		T		T
S	I	S	T	E		S	A	E	V	A

(This is not the only possible solution.)

8 Celebration time

```
C E N A ■ V I N U M ■ P O C U L A
S U P E R A T A ■ P U L S A N D A
H A U R I O ■ E U G E ■ L I T U S
A N T O N I U S ■ V I C T O R I A
A V E ■ B I B E ■ A E G Y P T U S
T R I U M P H U S ■ A G R I P P A
C L E O P A T R A ■ T U R P I U M
S O D A L E S ■ S E R P E N T E S
A R M A ■ N A V E S ■ R E G I N A
M O N S T R U M ■ A U G U S T U S
```

```
N U N C ■ E S T ■ B I B E N D U M
```

This quotation comes from Horace Odes I.37 and marks a time of celebration after Cleopatra's defeat.

9 Latin to English crossword

```
T O H A V E E A T E N
H ■ A ■ E ■ R ■ R ■ O
E N T E R S A T O M B
Y ■ E ■ Y ■ S ■ U ■ L
E ■ ■ ■ P E O P L E
X ■ H ■ T ■ S ■ S ■ F
P E E R I N ■ ■ ■ R
L ■ B ■ V ■ L ■ T ■ I
A H E R O T O S O M E
I ■ A ■ L ■ N ■ G ■ N
N O T H I N G G O O D
```

10 English to Latin crossword

```
■ I ■ C ■ L ■ E ■ P
I N C A P I T I B U S
■ T ■ L ■ N ■ ■ ■ G
B E L L A G R A T I A
■ L ■ I ■ U ■ D ■ O
G L A D I A T O R I S
■ E ■ U ■ D ■ R ■ P
E G I S T I F A L S A
■ E ■ ■ ■ G ■ T ■ I
B R I T A N N I C U S
■ E ■ U ■ A ■ S ■ S
```

11 Latin to Latin crossword

```
V A T E S ■ F I N I O
E ■ O ■ U N O ■ U ■ P
L A T U M ■ S I L V A
I ■ I ■ M O S ■ L ■ C
S I S T O ■ A V A R A
■ A ■ E ■ ■ A ■ U
U M B R A ■ A E D I S
L ■ R ■ D I E ■ I ■ I
U M E N S ■ G E R I T
L ■ V ■ I R E ■ U ■ U
O R E N T ■ R I S U M
```

12 Crazy, you must know

```
P A R S ■ G E N S
O ■ ■ R ■ ■ ■ U
N ■ A M E N S ■ N
S ■ R ■ G ■ C ■ T
■ L E G I T I S ■
T ■ N ■ T ■ T ■ E
R ■ A Q U A E ■ M
E ■ ■ R ■ ■ ■ I
S I V E ■ A D E S
```

13 Famous Romans: Cicero

```
A R P I N U M
 A N T O N Y
     V E R R E S
    T U L L I U S
     S I C I L Y
    C H I C K P E A
    C O N S U L
     M A R C U S
C O N C O R D I A
P O M P E Y
 T I R O
     A T T I C U S
   C A T I L I N E
```

The answer: NOVUS HOMO ERAT
(Cicero was an outsider to the world of Roman politics: a new man.)

14 Latin to English crossword

```
■ R ■ C ■ S ■ B E S T
W E F O R C E ■ V ■ I
■ F ■ L ■ A ■ S E E M
M U R D E R S ■ N ■ E
■ S ■ E ■ E ■ ■ I
W E A R E D I N I N G
■ S ■ B ■ E ■ F
M ■ D ■ W E O W N E D
I ■ T I S ■ A ■ W ■ V
N ■ N ■ I S T A Y E D
D I E S ■ T ■ Y ■ R
```

15 English to Latin crossword

```
■ V ■ T ■ L ■ A Q U A
N O B I L I S ■ U ■ N
■ C ■ M ■ B ■ P O S T
T A C E T I S ■ S ■ E
■ T ■ N ■ D ■ ■ P
S U N T F I D E L E S
■ S ■ ■ N ■ X ■ C
T ■ O ■ H O S T I U M
A L M A ■ S ■ U ■ N
L ■ N ■ P U E L L I S
E H E U ■ S ■ I ■ A
```

16 Latin to Latin crossword

17 The Roman way

This famous statement about Roman imperial values comes from Virgil's Aeneid I.279.

18 Latin to English crossword

19 English to Latin crossword

20 Latin to Latin crossword

21 Abbreviations Wordsearch

22 Famous Romans: Augustus

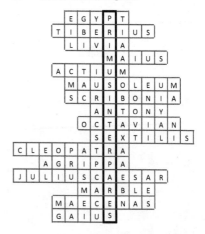

The answer: PRIMUS INTER PARES
(This is how Augustus wanted himself to be seen: the first among equals.)

76

23 Slowly does it

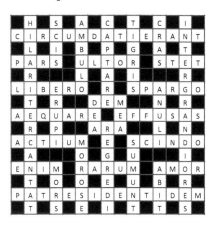

```
S A L . G . L E C T I
E . E . R E I . A . U
D E N S A . M O N E S
. T . D . E T . T . .
F R E Q U E N T A R E
. E . U . G . U . U .
E X C O G I T A T I S
B . E . E . O . O . .
R A N I S . R O G A T
I . A . S I S . A . A
A B E G I . I . S I M
```

24 Some things to do

```
Q U A E D A M . T A M
U T . . E . . R . U
E . D I S P A R A N T
R . A . I . S . N . A
I M P O S I T U S . T
. . I . T . R . F .
F . S U E T O N I U S
E . A . R . L . G . I
C O M M E M O R O . M
I . O . . G . . T U
T E R . A L I E N U S
```

25 Latin to English crossword

```
. T . C . E . A . B . A . H
Y O U H A V E B E E N S E E N
. C . A . E . A . H . K . A
F O R S T R A N G E R S . T O
. L . I . Y . D . A . O R .
B U R N E D . O L D . . U S E
. M . G . A . N . . I L L
O N E . B Y N I G H T . E N D
. . Y O U . N . E . W O .
S E E . T O L D . S T A R T S
. S O . F . A . H . S . A
O N . . I S I N L O Y A L T Y
. E . B . T . G . U . M . A
E X P O S E S E N T R A I L S
. T . Y . P . R . S . N . L
```

26 English to Latin crossword

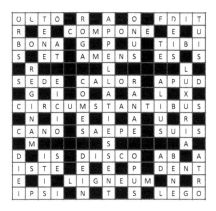

```
. H . S . A . C . T . C . I
C I R C U M D A T I E R A N T
. L . I . B . P . G . A . T
P A R S . U L T O R . S T E T
. R . . L . A . I . . . R
L I B E R O . R . S P A R G O
. T . R . D E M . . N . R
A E Q U A R E . E F F U S A S
. R . P . A R A . L . N
A C T I U M . E . S C I N D O
. A . . O . G . U . . . I
E N I M . R A R U M . A M O R
. T . O . O . E . U . B . R
P A T R E S I D E N T I D E M
. T . S . E . I . T . T . S
```

27 Latin to Latin crossword

```
O L T O . R . A . O . F N I T
R . E . C O M P O N E . E . U
B O N A . G . P . U . T I B I
S . E T . A M E N S . E S . S
. R . . . L . . . . . L
S E D E . C A L O R . A P U D
G . I . O . A . A . L . X
C I R C U M S T A N T I B U S
. N . I . E . I . A . U . R
C A N O . S A E P E . S U I S
. M . . . S . . . . . A
D . I S . D I S C O . A B . A
I S T E . E . E . P . D E N T
E . I . L I G N E U M . N . R
I P S I . N . T . S . L E G O
```

28 A Roman whodunnit

The answer is Marcus. The first letter of each sentence spells out his name. (Specta primum!)

29 It's difficult

```
C U B I C U L U M
A . . . A . . . U
L . A R C E M . L
E . D . H . A . I
D I F F I C I L E
O . L . N . U . B
N . O M N I S . R
I . . . A . . . I
A C C U S A T U S
```

30   Latin to English crossword

```
  A   C   P U T   F   W
S C R O L L   A G R E E D
  R   M   O A K   I   S
H O N E S T   E J E C T S
  S   T   S I N   N   O
I S N O T   N   A D E P T
L   E   E X A C T   Y   R
L A T I N   L   E N E M Y
  C   M   O L D   O   A
S C H O O L   E N T E R S
  E   U   D I N   I   K
S P A R S E   S I N G E R
  T   N   R U E   G   T
```

31   English to Latin crossword

```
  E   R   C   B   S   D
A Q U A   A V E   A F U I
  U   R U S   N O N   R
V I R I   A G E   E R I T
  T   U   E   P   O
M I N O R   R   R U E R E
    O   B R E V E   X
P O S S E   B   M A I O R
  B   M   A   E   B
I S T A   E M E   A L I A
  T   C U R   S E D   E
D A R E   R E S   D I C O
  S   R   O   E   O   I
```

32   Latin to Latin crossword

```
  R   P   N O S   O   A
R E C E D O   A P P O N E
  D   T   V I X   I   T
F I D E L E   I G N O R O
  T   R   M O S   O   U
A U D E S   R   P R E M O
U   U   I M B R E   A   R
T A C E T   E   S U M M A
  V   X   A M A   S   U
V I N C A M   E Q U I T O
  D   U   E S T   R   A
F O R S A N   A S P E R E
  S   O   S I S   O   E
```

33   Sudoku

VII	III	VI	V	IX	IV	II	I	VIII
IX	VIII	I	II	III	VI	IV	VII	V
IV	II	V	VII	I	VIII	III	VI	IX
VIII	V	VII	IV	VI	III	I	IX	II
I	IV	IX	VIII	II	V	VI	III	VII
II	VI	III	IX	VII	I	VIII	V	IV
III	IX	II	I	VIII	VII	V	IV	VI
V	I	VIII	VI	IV	IX	VII	II	III
VI	VII	IV	III	V	II	IX	VIII	I

34   Famous Romans: Nero

```
DOMUSAUREA
CLAUDIUS
BRITANNICUS
BURRUS
POPPAEA
ANTIUM
VINDEX
SENECA
BOUDICCA
GREATFIRE
OCTAVIA
AGRIPPINA
SUETONIUS
```

The answer: MATREM NECAVIT
(This refers to the murder of Nero's mother Agrippina.)

35   Unwanted

```
  P   P   H   S I   B
N O L E B A N T   M E
  S   R   B   A T   N
E S T   V I S   S E
  U   Q   T   N   T
A M B U L A B A M U S
  U   O   V   M   L
E S   E I S   I T A
X   T U S   I
I N   N I T I D I O R
T   D A   I   O   R
```

36 Latin to English crossword

	C		B		S		W		A		R	
W	H	E	R	E	W	E	R	E	T	H	E	Y
	A		E		E		I		L		T	
I	N		E		E	A	T		A		U	S
	G		Z		T		T		S		R	
W	E	W	E	R	E	M	E	E	T	I	N	G
	D				R		N				P	
E	N	E	M	Y	S	O	L	D	I	E	R	S
	A		O		M		E		N		O	
I	T		T	H	E	A	T	R	E		U	P
	U		I		L		T		A		D	
T	R	A	V	E	L	W	E	A	R	I	L	Y
	E		E		S		R		S		Y	

37 English to Latin crossword

	C		G		A		F		U			I
C	O	L	L	A	T	A	E	E	R	A	N	T
	N		O		R		L		B		G	
A	V	E	R	T	O		E	L	I	G	E	T
	O		I		S	I	S		U		N	
S	C	I	A	M		L		E	M	O	T	A
	A		E	T	I	A	M				I	
A	V	A	R	A		U		I	U	S	S	I
	I		E		A	M	A		R		S	
A	S	I	N	U	S		B	R	E	V	I	S
	S		O		I		E		N		M	
P	E	R	V	I	A	M	A	R	D	U	A	M
	T		O		M		M		O		M	

38 Latin to Latin crossword

	I		A		D		A		M		C	
I	N	S	C	R	I	P	T	I	O	N	E	S
	T		R		S		T		R		N	
U	R	S	I		C	U	I		O	R	A	E
	A		O		E		N		S		T	
I	N	G	R	E	D	I	E	B	A	T	U	R
	T				E		R				R	
A	M	P	H	I	T	H	E	A	T	R	U	M
	E		I		A		P		E		M	
A	D	D	E		C	U	R		R	U	E	S
	I		M		I		I		R		S	
S	C	R	I	P	T	U	M	S	E	N	S	I
	I		S		E		A		O		E	

39 A Roman riddle

The answer is a *Mars Bar*. The first letter of the riddle is *m*, then *a* is the first letter of all, *r* is the middle letter of *cerae*, and *s* is the last bit of *finis*. After that, you have to add a *taberna*, or *bar*.

40 Latin to English crossword

H	I	L	L	S		A	G	A	I	N
U	S			W		S			T	O
G		T	H	A	N	K	E	D		T
E		O		R		I		E		E
R	E	N	O	M	I	N	A	T	E	D
		I		B		R		A		
B	E	G	G	R	E	E	T	I	N	G
O		H		I		T		N		R
U		T	O	N	G	U	E	S		A
N	O			G		R			A	S
D	R	O	P	S		N	E	S	T	S

41 English to Latin crossword

	U		E		E				C	
A	R	I	D	I		T	E	C	U	M
	S		U		E		P		R	
	A	R	C	E	S	S	I	V	I	
M	E		T		T		S		A	B
		M	I	S	C	E	T	E		
T	U		S		A		U		A	D
	S	C	U	R	R	I	L	E	S	
	Q		N		A		A		I	
M	U	L	T	O		T	E	M	N	O
	E		B		E				I	

42 Latin to Latin crossword

	O		I		T		E		L	
A	B	U	N	D	A	N	T	I	A	E
	M		E		M		I		E	
Q	U	A	S	I		C	A	S	T	A
	T		T	U	T	U	M		I	
S	E	D		B		P		E	S	T
	S		V	E	L	I	M		S	
S	C	I	A	S		S	A	T	I	S
	E		E		P		G		M	
G	R	A	M	M	A	T	I	C	U	M
	E		E		R		S		M	

43 Let it come

	S		L	I	B	E	T		P	
A	E	T	A	S		T	O	T	U	S
	R		E			L		R		
A	M	A	T	A		A	L	I	A	M
D	O		A	D	F	L	O		M	E
D			E		T				T	
A	T		T	A	C	E	T		D	A
M	O	V	E	T		R	E	G	A	M
	G		N			N		T		
E	A	D	E	M		R	E	B	U	S
	M		S	E	D	E	T		M	

44   Famous Romans: Hadrian

```
        T R A J A N
    P L O T I N A
    A N T O N I N U S
          M A T I D I A
      A E L I U S
        I T A L I C A
          P A N T H E O N
          T I V O L I
          S A B I N A
        A U G U S T A
  A N T I N O U S
            L I M E S
          A T H E N S
```

The answer: ANIMULA VAGULA
(This was Hadrian's poem about his own little wandering spirit.)

45   Latin to English crossword

```
    D   T   I   T   D   S
  S E C O N D T H O U G H T
    L   E   I   I   S   E
  D I E S   O D E   T O W N
    V   I T   F       I
  N E V E R   N   U N C L E
    R     O P E N S     L
  S E V E N   W   E L B O W
    D     C   U S     F
  A L A S   R A N   R A F T
    A   E   O   D   U   E
  T W O N E W L E G I O N S
    S   D   D   R   N   D
```

46   English to Latin crossword

```
    I   S   D   I   F   M
  I N S C R I P T I O N I S
    T   I   S   E   R   N
  G E N S   C O R   E X I T
    M       I   C       M
  O P U S A D H I B I T U M
    E   I   I   C   U   S
  F R A C T U M E X S E C O
    A       M   R       U
  E N I M   R U O   R A R A
    T   O   U   N   E   R
  P E R D I F F I C I L I S
    R   O   I   S   S   T
```

47   Latin to Latin crossword

```
    F   O   R   S   U   I
  Q U A M C E L E R R I M E
    G   N   G   X   B   P
  B I B E   I I T   S T E T
    T   E A   A T     R
  L I B E R   A   E T I A M
    V     A G M E N     T
  Q U I E S   O   D O L O R
    S     I S   D O     R
  C E P I   O D I   O P E S
    H   N   C V   M   R
  A E D I F I C A V E R A M
    U   S   I   E   N   T
```

48   Latin to English crossword

```
    L   A   N   S   F   S   P
  M O S T B E A U T I F U L L Y
    A   O   E   S   G   N   A
  S T O P   D I T C H   S A Y S
    H     L   A   T       C
  E S T A T E   I   S I N G L E
    O   R   A N D   U   E
  I M M O R A L   I M P R O V E
    E   S   L E G   S   E
  O B J E C T   S   S P E A R S
    E     H   C   O     G
  L A N D   R O A D S   D R A G
    S   E   O   P   O   A   M
  I T H A S B E E N F O R C E D
    S   F   S   S   T   E   S
```

49   English to Latin crossword

```
    O   C   L   H   C   E   I
  I M P U N I T I F U E R A N T
    N   R   C   S   R   I   T
  R I P A   T A C E S   T R E S
    B       O   A   U       R
  S U F F E R   R   S T A T I M
    S   L   A E S   M   N
  A D L O Q U I   I N C E S S I
    I   R   T A M   N   T
  S C R I B I   L   I N S E R O
    E   N   I   N       U
  I N D E   C A E C A   V I C I
    D   X   E   N   U   I   T
  I U S T E P R O G R E D I O R
    M   A   I   S   A   I   S
```

50 Latin to Latin crossword

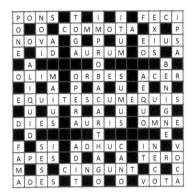

51 Diamond words

```
        M
       M I
      S I M
     E M I S
    M I S E R
   T R E M I S
  M I S E R A T
 M A G I S T E R
  R E G A T I S
   I T E R A S
    S T A R E
     E R A S
      R E S
       S E
        E
```

52 Diamond words

```
        A
       E A
      V A E
     D E V A
    E V A D O
   D E V O R A
  A D V E R T O
 D E V I A T O R
  D E R I V A T
   V E T A R I
    V E R T I
     V E R I
      V I R
       V I
        V
```

53 Diamond words

```
        E
       M E
      E M O
     T E M O
    T I M E O
   O P T I M E
  I M P E T R O
 I M P L O R E T
  T E M P O R I
   P R E M I T
    P E R I T
     R I T E
      I R E
       E I
        I
```

54 Six all round

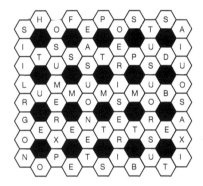

55 Six all round

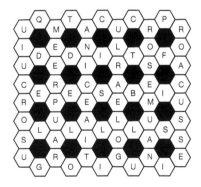

56 Six all round

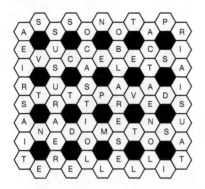

57 Double trouble - expose envy

58 Double trouble

59 Double trouble

60 Home for prayers

DARETIS
TRADES
SEDAT
ADES
DEA
DE
SED
EDAS
AEDES
REDEAS
DESERTA

NOVISTI
VISITO
VOTIS
OVIS
VIS
IS
SUI
RUIS
PRIUS
PRIMUS
ERUMPIS

61 Fools to dance

TULISTI
STULTI
LITUS
SITU
UTI
UT
AUT
RUAT
TAURI
ATRIUM
RUMINAT

DIRECTA
ADIRET
RETIA
RATE
TER
ET
EAT
TALE
ALTER
RELATA
SALTARE

62 Poor rotter

GESTIRE
TIGRES
REGIS
GERI
EGI
EI
IRE
REMI
MISER
REMISI
GREMIIS

SUPERAT
REPUTA
PUTER
RUPE
PER
RE
ORE
ERRO
MORER
RUMORE
HORREUM

63 Arrowword

	P		R		S		A		A		P
T	I	M	E	N	T		D	E	B	E	O
	U		O		E	L	I	G	O		N
E	S	U	R	I	R	E		O	L	E	T
	S				T	O	T		E	M	E
E	Q	U	I	T	O			I	S	I	S
	U		T			C	U	R			T
C	O	G	A	T			U	E	S	T	E
	E		O	D	I			M	E	O	S
V	I	R	A	G	O				R		S
	N	O	T	A		C	E	N	A	R	E
	V		R		S	U	M	E		E	
N	A	V	I	S		R	O	G	A	T	E
	D	I	U		E	A		A	V	I	S
P	E	R	M	I	T	T	O		E	A	T

64 Arrowword

	R		C		C		P		I		Q
B	E	N	E		E		A	R	S		U
	V		L	E	N	I	R	E		S	E
C	O	R	O	N	A		O	S	S	I	S
	C		S	T	O			A	S	T	
V	A	E		I	I		E	L		U	
	T	U	S	S	I	R	E		E	S	
O	S		L		N	A	S		X		
	P	T	E		I	S	T	I	U	S	
D	E	F	E	N	D	I			O	R	E
	C	U	R			T	U		C	O	R
A	T	R	I	U	M		R	E	A		V
	A		O	B		A	S		R	U	I
S	T	O	R	I	A		E	V	I	T	O

65 Arrowword

	I		E		A			E		D		V		
	T	U	T	O	R		I	S	E		V	E	R	
	A		S	C	I	E	N	T	I	A		R	E	
E	Q	U	I	T	E	S		O	B	E	A	T	I	S
T	U		O	S	S	A		L		T	E			
E	G	O		E	G	I		S	I		A	S		
R		M	E		E	S	S	E	T		I	S		
G	R	A	T	I	A		T	E	N	E	T		P	
A	C		M	A	L	A		T	R	E	M	O		
E	T	I	A	M		T		E		R	E	S		
I	L	L	E		P	A	E	N	E		I	T		
C	O	I	T	U	S		A	B	I	T		O	S	
S	E	M	P	E	R		I	S				P		
V		R		E	S	S	E	D	A		D	I	E	
V	I	R		A	S	T		S	I		M	O	N	S

83

ALSO AVAILABLE
LATIN AND GREEK PUZZLE BOOKS

These collections are aimed at those who want to have some fun with the Latin and ancient Greek languages they know and love. All of these books feature solutions at the back for those who get stuck.

Easy Latin Puzzles was written after compiling three lists of words commonly used in a variety of Latin courses. It makes very limited use of word endings and includes a variety of challenges, including sudokus, word searches, Latin to English crosswords and English to Latin ones. The latest edition of the book has been expanded to include 60 puzzles as well as comprehensive word lists at the back.

Easy Greek Puzzles is a set of 60 brainteasers, improved and extended from the original edition, with 10 entirely new puzzles and accents incorporated for the first time. The book was first assembled from two short lists of words commonly used in a variety of beginners' courses and uses all five cases of noun, adjective and pronoun systems, as well as the active indicative verb endings from the present, imperfect, aorist and future tenses. It is appropriate for use by those who have studied the language for around one year or longer.

Tricky Greek Puzzles was written for those whose command of ancient Greek may allow them to enjoy its challenges - not for the faint-hearted. It includes 50 crosswords, sudokus, wordsearches and other brainteasers and is aimed at those who have studied the language for two or three years at least.

QUARE ID FACIAM

Nil nisi latinum, nil nisi quod Cicero ipse resolvere potuisset.

Centum ludi verbis latinis in hoc libro compositi sunt in quibus gaudium et quietem e tempestate invenire possis. Inter aenigmata sunt verba transversa, favi, sagittae, coniunctis quaerendis, numeratis numerandis, novomnia, verbomnia, hodierna latinata, verba instructa.

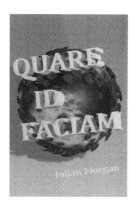

Centum aenigmata sunt in libro sed si diligentius respicias, fortasse unum insuper videas. Si hoc aenigma CI repertum confeceris, nomen tuum in nostrum album optimatium in texto referetur.

"Si hoc intellegis...
Si lingua latina te delectat...
Si ludi cum verbis tibi oblectationem praebent...

Tibi hic liber est!"
Stephen Jenkin, The Classics Library

SONNETS FOR CLASSICAL STARS

This book was written as a follow-up companion to our earlier volume of poems, *Sonnets for Yorkshire Stars*. It contains 100 poems about leading figures in the ancient world, from the mythological to the historical, the literary to the artistic. The split in the book is roughly 50-50 Greek to Roman and the list of names included contains Poseidon, Homer, Nero and even Lesbia. The four main categories of the classical stars are Sagas and Stories, Sanctuaries and Shrines, Skill and Style and State and Standing. Highly recommended for the more poetic sort of classicist.

"Here are sonnets as history essays, as digests of the past, as mini encyclopedias and as rhyming invitations to explore further. So enjoy, and explore further!"
Ian McMillan

CLASSICAL PUZZLES

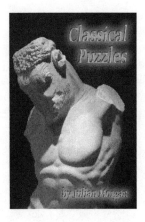

Classical Puzzles is a collection of brainteasers which focuses on the literature, culture and history of the ancient world rather than its languages. There are many people fascinated by classical civilisation who have not studied Latin and Greek and up until now, they may have been denied some fun: this book is an attempt to put that right and to complement our existing range of Latin and Greek puzzle books, not to mention the Yorkshire ones. This collection will test your knowledge of the Greeks and Romans with crosswords, sudokus and all kinds of wordgames to challenge you. Go on, test yourself out.

Can you separate your Caesars from your Ciceros? Your Spartans from your Athenians? It's all here: from art and architecture to geography, from politics to literature, from history to myths; a cornucopia of classical civilisation!

ROMAN BRITAIN PUZZLES

Britannia's the game

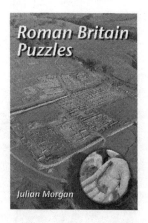

How well do you know Roman Britain? You'll soon find out, if you take on these 50 assorted crosswords and brainteasers. Caesar, Claudius and Hadrian all feature, as do sites from Vindolanda to Bignor, from Caerleon to Colchester. Roads, villas, artwork and inscriptions will test you to the max. Don't worry though - all the answers are in the back!

"These puzzles will provide great fun for the casual student of Roman Britain and will even challenge the experts in places."

Barbara Birley, The Vindolanda Trust

IMPERIUM LATIN COURSE

The Imperium Latin course has been written for the twenty-first century; unique, highly resourced and written to make fullest use of modern technology. Its texts follow the life of the Emperor Hadrian from his early childhood to his later years, as he became the most powerful man in the Roman world.

Imperium was released for general use in 2013, after a trialling period of six years. It consists of three course books, a Grammar and Syntax book, a puzzle book and the Imperium Latin Unseens collection for advanced users. All of these texts can be ordered through Amazon but are also available as pdf files in our Site Support Packs, which can be bought by schools. The three course books are also available as free of charge downloadable pdf files, from the TES Resources website.

"Much thought and effort has gone into keeping the course rigorous and quick-paced, without overwhelming or discouraging students. The amount of assistance and supplemental material available to teachers as they present this course is truly remarkable."

Sharon Kazmierski, Classical Outlook, Fall 2013

A SERIES OF YORKSHIRE PUZZLES

There are three books in the Yorkshire Puzzles series. Each one boasts 50 puzzles, including crosswords and other types of word-games written to test your knowledge of the county. Don't expect to find them easy unless you are an expert on Yorkshire dialect, cricket, brass bands, geography, history... and so the list goes on.

What they said about the first book in the series:

"Aimed at the more knowledgeable reader, this volume is filled with tough questions that will challenge even the most ardent Yorkshirephiles."

Dalesman, February 2017

SONNETS FOR YORKSHIRE STARS

The poems in this collection have been written to celebrate 100 of the county's outstanding achievers. The list of their names was compiled carefully to reflect all aspects of life, so you'll find artists, musicians, politicians, sporting personalities and writers here: Yorkshire's finest, all celebrated in fourteen-line verse.

"So honoured that you chose to write of me and am delighted it was in the form of a poem and not a puzzle! Warmest good wishes."   Baroness Betty Boothroyd

"Many thanks. Very interesting to read about my fellow Yorkshire folk."   Dickie Bird

"Perfectly crafted stories that brim with rhythm and dance with rhyme."   Ian McMillan

"I feel flattered to be portrayed in verse."

Peter Wright, The Yorkshire Vet

WORLD OF JAMES HERRIOT PUZZLES

Fans of the world's most famous vet, pencils at the ready! This collection was made in collaboration with the World of James Herriot in Thirsk and includes 50 puzzles, based on all eight books of the famous vet's memoirs as well as on-screen depictions, including the BBC series *All creatures great and small.*

Animals and ailments, colleagues and customers, potions and powders of the original books of memoirs are all here, as well as on-screen portrayals of vets and locations, both real and fictional. Don't worry though. If it all gets too much, the solutions are in the back.

"This volume of puzzles comes from the pen of Yorkshire Author Julian Morgan and closely matches the content of the books written by James Herriot. The challenges posed vary from simple wordsearch to cryptic conundrum and will surely appeal to Herriot fans of all ages. Julian's puzzles are respectful in adhering to the original stories and will bring new ways for readers to connect again with the stories they love."

Ian Ashton, Managing Director, World of James Herriot

CITY OF YORK PUZZLES

This collection will provide hours of amusement for fans of our great county town, boasting 50 assorted crosswords and challenging word-games of various types. Facets of history, arts, attractions, streets, famous faces, sports, pubs and shops all feature, so if you love York, you should love what's on offer here.

Not for the faint-hearted, it's a good job you can find the answers in the back. So go on, how well do you know York?

ABOUT THE AUTHOR

Julian Morgan served as a teacher and a Head of Classics for many years in the UK and in Germany. Julian has now stepped down from classroom teaching and is very happy to be living in his native Yorkshire once again.

Julian has written a wide range of educational software titles and books in the last 35 years, publishing many of these under the banner of his business, J-PROGS. His Imperium Latin course is used in a good number of schools and can be downloaded free of charge by following the links from www.imperiumlatin.com. He is a member of the *O Tempora!* crossword setting team for The Times newspaper and the puzzle master for ARGO magazine.

He can often be found walking his dog in the Great Wold Valley of North Yorkshire, where he lives.

To find out more, see www.j-progs.com

Twitter feed: @imperiumlatin

Made in the USA
Las Vegas, NV
28 November 2023

81739181R00057